HOME SWAPPING

HELEN KAULBACH

 FriesenPress

One Printers Way
Altona, MB R0G 0B0
Canada

www.friesenpress.com

ISBN
978-1-03-915510-7 (Hardcover)
978-1-03-915509-1 (Paperback)
978-1-03-915511-4 (eBook)

1. TRAVEL, AUSTRALIA & OCEANIA

Distributed to the trade by The Ingram Book Company

DOUGLAS KAULBACH 1934 - 2022

Home Swapping is lovingly dedicated to Doug, who was very much a part of this adventure. He lived every day of it with me. He encouraged me to write the story and added some of his own recollections.

Sadly, he did not survive to see the finished product, but it is as much his story as mine.

THANK YOU

Thank you to the exchange couples who gave me permission to use their names in this book.

The ones I no longer had contact information for, or who did not answer my query, were not identified. I used instead, names or initials that were not their own.

Thank you to all the people whose homes we stayed in and enjoyed. I hope you enjoyed our home as much as we enjoyed yours.

And a special thank you to all the friends and neighbours of our exchange couples, who welcomed us so warmly and made our visit so special.

Thank you also to Jack Graber of Homelink Canada who was always available to answer any questions.

The years we spent Home Exchanging, travelling to far-flung places, meeting great people and learning about other cultures, were some of our happiest years and created memories that will live forever.

H.K.

TABLE OF CONTENTS

Chapter 1

HOME SWAPPING, WHY WE DO IT

ON A HOT DAY in February my husband, Doug, and I, were relaxing on the terrace of a waterfront condo watching the surfers enjoying the waves and the beach on Australia's Sunshine Coast. Back home in Canada it was below freezing, but we were enjoying a one-month holiday in Australia that was completely different from anything we'd done before.

We were staying in a luxury two-level penthouse apartment in one of Australia's premier vacation areas. The apartment had seven terraces including a rooftop terrace with a hot tub.

During our stay there we drove a sporty Renault SUV and travelled all over central Queensland.

We were invited to a private home up in the hills for a real "Australian Barbie", where we met some really interesting people. Two of those people we arranged to meet again the next summer on another trip to England.

Doug played golf several times at a private golf club.

And I was invited to a luncheon meeting of the local University Women's Club.

Are we rich, you ask? Not by a long shot! We're retired and living on a pension.

That marvellous holiday cost us only our airfare – and we even got a deal on that, booking online at 30% off.

We can afford such luxurious holidays, not just once, but two or three times a year because we're members of a Home Exchange Club.

In the next 12 years after that first exchange, we did 18 home swaps. We often put together two or three exchanges in one trip, especially if the exchange involved a long flight such as Australia or New Zealand.

Home exchanges have been around for a long time, but have seen a resurgence recently because of the high cost of accommodations and fluctuating currency rates in foreign countries.

We were so committed to home exchanging that we were only home from our first exchange to Australia for a week when we started planning our next trip, this one to Britain the following August, where we stayed in a suburban home in a small village just outside Manchester in the north of England. There we met all the neighbours, spent some time with them at the local pub and got to drive another car on the left side of the road.

The following winter we went back to Australia a second time. For this trip we put together three separate exchanges in three different places in Brisbane and the Gold Coast. One of them was a 25th floor oceanfront condo right on the beach near Surfer's Paradise. These were fabulous accommodations we could never have afforded to pay for. Another one was a suburban home in Brisbane with our own backyard pool, and great neighbours who invited us for dinner and to a local street party.

We've even done three exchanges closer to home, on Vancouver Island, BC. One of these was on the northern part of the Island and the other two were in the city of Victoria, BC's capital. These two weren't quite as exotic as the others but just as much fun as Victoria was a city we had never explored.

One of our more ambitious exchanges was a combination of two in Australia on separate coasts, in Perth and Melbourne, with a third in New Zealand. That trip we also added a three-day trip across the Nullorbor Desert on the Indian Pacific Railway, so we were away from home more than three months.

One of the best things about arranging home exchanges is that our house is occupied all the time we're away.

Our winter exchangers shovel snow from the driveway and keep the walkways clear. For some, mainly the Australians, this is a novelty as it's the first time they've done it. Our summer exchangers dead-head the roses, water the hanging baskets and enjoy anything we've planted such as tomatoes, salad greens or rhubarb.

This is the story of our 14 years of home swapping, the adventures (and misadventures) we've had, and the marvellous people we've met along the way.

Chapter 2

HOW IT'S DONE

WHEN WE FIRST STARTED, the exchange club had a printed directory, but today they are strictly on the internet.

The way it works is that once two exchangers make contact, they agree on the terms of the exchange; the most important being dates, whether a car is included and smoking or non-smoking.

Essentially, what you are exchanging is your home life and your lifestyle. You exchange your house, car and contents of the fridge. You also do chores like watering the plants and feeding the cat. Instead of a sterile hotel room you get comfortable chairs to watch TV in the evening, and a well-equipped kitchen when you feel like cooking. You'll get neighbours who will recommend places to go, and sometimes even take you there.

The house you get depends, of course, on the luck of the draw. We were really lucky with our oceanfront condos in Mooloolaba, Queensland, and on the Gold Coast. Our exchange couples got our two-bedroom house in a retirement community in Kelowna, which on the surface doesn't seem a fair exchange. But they were here to ski, and were happy with our home's warm coziness. The unfinished basement where the furnace is located gave them a place to dry their ski gear each night.

Part of the exchange deal is exchanging cars, and here they got the better deal. They got our GMC Envoy 4-wheel-drive, which they needed to drive to the ski hills. Most Australians that we met seemed to prefer their cars with standard shift and a stick-shift on the floor. I can tell you that sitting on the wrong side of the car, driving on the wrong side of the road and changing gears with the left hand, is very intimidating. We decided that only one of us (Doug) would drive while the other (me) would study the road map, navigate, watch the road signs and yell, "Keep Left" every 30 seconds. The combination worked because we survived our many trips and different cars without a scratch.

We've had many more offers, from all over the world, than we've been able to accept. We've had dozens of offers from Australia and New Zealand, several from Britain, a couple from Germany, a few from the US and even several from within Canada.

We've also realized that living in a resort area like Kelowna is a great asset for a home exchanger. We can exchange with either winter or summer visitors. Some want to come for the skiing and others for our beaches, wineries and golf courses.

We moved to Kelowna, BC, in 2000. That first winter we towed our travel trailer to Arizona and Nevada for two months. The next winter we wanted to do something different and when we saw an ad for a condo in Australia for six weeks with a combination price that included airfare and transfers, we went to see the travel agent. We booked it from mid-January to the end of February and when the agent suggested maximizing the airfare by adding a two-week bus tour in New Zealand, we agreed.

That trip was an epiphany. We loved Australia, we loved the people, we loved everything we saw. We wanted more. It put a hunger in our hearts for discovering new places.

However, all the sightseeing we did and adding the two-week bus tour drained our bank account. We quickly realized that being retired and living on a pension would not support that kind of life-style and if we wanted to travel, we had to do things differently.

We had heard about home swapping and even met someone once who had done it, so we started to do some research on the subject. We actually came up with five different companies that did online home exchanging and checked them all out. After going on all their sites, reading their mandates and checking their reviews, we settled on one with a Vancouver address. We felt more comfortable with a Canadian based company. That company was Homelink, and we later found out that they are worldwide in 20+ countries and the Vancouver address was only their Canadian agent. Regardless of our reasons for choosing them, it was the right choice for us. We did 16 successful exchanges over 9 years, dropped our membership for a couple of years due to health problems, rejoined again for two years and did two more exchanges.

We had only one major problem in all that time and Homelink really went to bat for us to resolve it. An exchange couple in Sydney, Australia, cancelled only three weeks before departure. That left us with a non-refundable airfare and nowhere to go. As it happened, we found another exchange for that time, not in Sydney, but in Brisbane. That exchange turned out to be one of our favorites. We loved the city of Brisbane and that couple are still our friends. We've met them twice more in other cities and are still in touch by e-mail and Christmas cards.

If we hadn't resolved this problem, we wouldn't have lost everything that we'd spent on this trip as Homelink has an insurance policy. A $25 fee (it might be a bit more by now) added to the annual fee covers out-of-pocket expenses if an exchange is cancelled unexpectedly. The annual fee for access to the website has changed a couple of times over the years, but is still no more than one night in a good hotel. Where else could you get one month's holiday accommodation for the price of one night?

With a lot of trepidation and not really knowing what to expect, in the spring of 2003 we signed up with Homelink. At that time, they had a printed directory as well as an online site. When the printed directory arrived, we spent a couple of weeks going through it and marking "possibles" in red, as well as putting paperclips on the pages of areas we were interested in.

We weren't in this directory, of course, but we were online. In our online profile we filled out the questionnaire, listing the type of house, number of bedrooms and bathrooms, nearby attractions, and any specific rules we had. Our specifications were: no smoking, no children and no pets. The no children clause was because we live in a seniors' age 55+ community with no facilities for children, and children, even grandchildren of residents, are not allowed in the clubhouse or pool. The no pets clause was because we don't have pets and one of the reasons we didn't want to look after a pet during our exchange was that we wanted to travel and do some sight-seeing while we were there, using the exchange home as a base. In that circumstance, a pet would be a problem.

We also took photos of the outside and inside of our house and posted those on our online profile.

Other specifics in our profile were dates (in our case, anytime) our preferred destinations (Australia, New Zealand, UK and USA). We also added "open" to our destination, as did many others, because something interesting might turn up unexpectedly.

In August 2003 we were screwing up our courage to contact a couple of exchange possibilities in the Sydney area in Australia, when a disaster hit our city that took away all thoughts of exchanging our house, as for a while we were in danger of losing it. A lightning strike in a park just outside the city limits ignited a wildfire that soon roared out of control towards a populated area. In the next few days 238 homes burned and live embers were being blown into the rest of the city including our backyard. Over the next week it burned across the hills behind the city, away from the homes, but cloaking the city in smoke and ash. A couple of our friends lost their homes and others were evacuated and unable to go back for several days. Our winter holiday was the last thing on our minds.

Toward the end of this "week of hell" two positive things happened. Our son, Pete, came to visit, bringing with him a new girlfriend named Natalie. We liked her immediately and told Pete that she was a keeper. He obviously thought so too as she is now our daughter-in-law and the mother of our two precious granddaughters.

The other positive happening that week was our first home exchange offer. A couple from Queensland, Australia, wanted to come to Kelowna for six weeks to ski at our local ski resort, Big White. We accepted, and that began our love affair with Australia and its people, and the start of a 14-year adventure spanning the globe.

Chapter 3

AUSTRALIA HERE WE COME —
MOOLOOLABA, QUEENSLAND

IN EARLY SEPTEMBER, 2003, we received our first home exchange offer. It was not Sydney, but our second choice, Queensland's Sunshine Coast, quite close to where we had stayed the previous year.

> *Dear Doug and Helen:*
>
> *Would you be interested in an exchange for six weeks next February 1 to March 15? We have been to Kelowna before and skied at Big White so know it well. We hope these dates suit you as we find January in the Okanagan far too cold and prefer the warmer weather in February and especially the spring skiing in March.*
>
> *We have a two level apartment with a rooftop terrace across the road from a beach in Mooloolaba, on the Sunshine Coast in Queensland. Check our site #***** for photos.*
>
> *Regards*
>
> *G & R*

We answered immediately, delighted with our first exchange offer. We were a little apprehensive with starting something completely new, but looking forward to our next adventure.

Dear G & R

Your e-mail was a welcome ray of sunshine after a scary and smoky summer. We have been plagued with wildfires that destroyed over 200 homes and threatened many others. Now that we know our home is safe we would be happy to accept your offer of six weeks, February 1 to March 15, 2004. We are also interested in the car exchange. Ours is a 4WD SUV which should handle the road to Big White easily.

Attached is our signed exchange agreement. We also have a fax if that makes it easier to send yours.

Cheers

Helen and Doug

The e-mail below was the start of many over the next five months. We passed on details such as where to pick up keys, our local contact's name and phone number, any condo rules where they live that might affect us, our times of arrival and flight numbers, and details of local happenings. We also added photos and personal details to get to know one another. By the time we actually travelled we felt we knew them well.

Dear Helen and Doug

We know all about wildfires as Australia has a very dry climate and is also susceptible to them. Also, G's brother-in-law is a firefighter. We read about your wildfire on the news and wondered if it affected you. Could you send me your fax number? I will fax both the exchange agreement and the car agreement within the week.

Regards

R

We never actually got to meet G & R. They flew into Kelowna on the same plane that we flew out on. We exchanged details on what we looked like and what we would probably be wearing, so were able to wave at one another through the glass that separated the arrivals from the departures.

Crossing paths that way made it easy to arrange travel to and from the airport.

The condo in Mooloolaba, our first home exchange, probably spoiled us for some of the others. It was a two-level apartment, three if you included the rooftop terrace. Each level had a terrace front and back. The upper level also had a large open area off the kitchen with a barbecue and table with umbrella. It was huge. Each level was as big as our whole house. The view from the front terrace was astounding; a long sweeping beach with a headland and lighthouse in the distance.

It was here that we came across a phenomenon that plagued us on many exchanges and we're sure that visitors to our home have had the same problem. Household appliances in foreign countries don't always work the same as ours. In North America, we travel back and forth between Canada and the United States quite frequently and our appliances all work seamlessly. But in Australia and New Zealand, Britain or Europe, all bets are off on appliances working as we would expect. In this case it was the kitchen cooktop. It was a ceramic cooktop set into the counter and I couldn't get it to stay on. I'd turn the dial, a light would come on, nothing else would happen and within about 30 seconds the light would go off. No heat. The instruction booklet in a drawer had detailed instructions for cleaning off different kinds of spills and warnings about scratching. It even had instructions on how to set the child-lock. Thinking that was the problem, we locked and unlocked it, but still no heat. Luckily, the instruction booklet had the name and address of the dealer where it was purchased, so off we went to visit the store. There we learned that it was an electromagnetic cooktop that required a stainless-steel pot with about an inch of water in it placed on the burner before turning it on. The pot of water completed the magnetic circuit and heated the water, not the cooktop, which apparently remained cool although I never tested it. The good thing about it was that the water started to boil in just a few seconds, far faster than any other stove I had ever used. I have since seen and used such cooktops elsewhere, but that was my first encounter with one.

After unpacking and doing our first grocery shopping, the next thing we did was look for the nearest RSL club. The RSL club (for Returned Service League) is roughly equivalent to our Legion, but with much more activity. Any retired or former member of any branch of the Armed Forces can join. But we also found out on our first trip there that visitors from another country were welcome to join for a monthly fee. The first time we joined it was $5.00, but in later years it was up to $10.00. Whatever it was, it was well worth it. Twice a week was Roast Night, usually Sunday and Wednesday. On our early trips it was $5 each and on later trips it was up to $8.00. For this we got a roast dinner, choice of beef, pork or lamb, with vegetables, a bowl of soup, dessert and coffee or tea. At those prices, we went often. The RSL was also a hub of activity on other nights. Twice a week there was Bingo, which is totally different from our bingo. Every night there was entertainment of some sort: a band for dancing, a comedian or a singer. One night a week was games night with all sorts of prizes. One night a week there was a meat draw. And then there were The Pokies. The Pokies are poker machines or slot machines, and these are the real money-makers that fund the clubs' benefits programs for returned and wounded veterans. For our modest monthly fee we had a wealth of entertainment.

One night at the RSL, about two weeks into our stay, we won a meat draw. There were three trays available that night, one each of pork, lamb and seafood. We won the lamb tray. I had no idea what I was going to do with it as I had never cooked lamb. That was a meat we only ever ate when ordering it in restaurants. When the draw was over, I overheard the lady who won the pork tray saying, "Oh, I so wish I had won the lamb." In seconds I was over at her table with my lamb tray offering to trade. She was so happy. So was I. The pork tray we got consisted of a large pork roast, large enough that I cut it in two roasts, two pork tenderloins, six chops, about two pounds of ground pork and a dozen sausages. Repackaged and put in the freezer, it fed us for most of the rest of our stay.

There was also a Surf Lifesaving Club near our apartment. Surf Clubs are a big deal in Australia. They started out as life saving clubs, and this is still their main purpose. Every morning, shortly after sunrise, we would see club members on the beach doing group exercises, running on the sand, practising life saving techniques, and launching the large wooden lifeboats and rowing them out beyond the surf line and back again. Most of this was simply to keep in shape for the monthly surf boat competitions as the actual life saving, if anyone was in trouble in the water, was done using motorized Sea Doos.

The Surf Clubs are also where children learn to swim. At age four or five, they join the Nipper program where they learn to swim, progressing through the age groups and eventually competing in swim meets with the other Surf Clubs. Some later go on to become lifeguards on the beach or join the Life-Savers. Each club has its own uniquely coloured or patterned swim cap, so watchers can identify their own swimmers during a competition.

The Surf Clubs are not membership clubs but open to the public for drinking and dining, and of course, playing the Pokies. The Surf Club dining rooms usually have specialty nights during the week. One night will be spaghetti night, the next seafood night, etc. We went one week on seafood night and there was a choice of a hot or cold seafood platter. We ordered one of each and shared them both, the hot first and then the cold. There were also salads and vegetables available on a buffet, but we didn't bother with those, just gorged on the seafood. We noticed later that most couples were sharing one platter.

One thing we found out is that home exchanging is not all fun and games as in vacationing at a resort where someone else solves any problems. If you're living in someone else's house and you have a problem, you do as you would at home – fix the problem. And if you can't fix it yourself you find someone who can.

The condo in Mooloolaba had a bright light over the dining room table, but it was on a dimmer switch, so we often dimmed it. One night as I was turning the dimmer knob I smelled something strange and then noticed a small waft of smoke coming from the switch. I immediately hit the OFF button and shut the light off. We discussed what to do, but as the smell went away with the light off and there was no more smoke, we decided to wait until morning. I have to admit that I checked that switch several times during the evening, feeling it for heat, and even got up in the night and checked it.

The next morning we went through the information binder left by the owners and found the "in case of emergency" sheet. One of the numbers listed was for an electrician, so we called him. When he removed the switch box from the wall it was blackened and sooty. The electrician said that dimmers often overheated and he would prefer to put in a simple ON/OFF switch for now and discuss replacing the dimmer switch when the owners returned. We agreed and that's what he did.

One other thing that happened while we were at that condo was a cyclone. We had experienced hurricanes several times on the Atlantic coast of North America, but this was our first experience with the Pacific equivalent. We had several days warning as the cyclone made its way down the coast, and our new local friends said not to worry as it happens all the time. They advised us not to leave anything loose on the terrace that might blow away or tip over. We brought all the chairs and small tables inside, and upended the tables too big to bring in. One large table that was fastened to the floor of the largest terrace with an attached umbrella, we couldn't do anything about. We thought it had been installed to weather any storm as it was too big to move, so left it alone. However, it was to cause us our biggest problem and the most dangerous to solve.

When the storm started, the wind-driven rain started running in under the glass terrace doors and under windows elsewhere. We spent most of the hours at the height of the storm running around from windows to doors with bath towels, stuffing them into window sills and door tracks to sop up the water and keep it from running across the floor. We're glad we never lost power as we soon ran out of dry towels and had the dryer going most of the time to keep up.

In the middle of all this, we noticed the big umbrella whipping in the wind and starting to rip. It was tied in two places, but that obviously wasn't enough. I raided the closet and found scarves and belts, as well as some of our own, and Doug went out in the raging storm to save the umbrella. He had to climb up and stand on the table, tighten the fabric and tie it starting at the bottom and every few inches as high as he could reach. He was soaked to the skin when he came back in.

When the storm started to let up, we were exhausted and sat by the window to watch the wind bending the trees and whipping up the waves on the beach. It was a fascinating sight. As the storm passed over and the sun came out, it seemed that everyone in town suddenly appeared on the beaches with surfboards and boogie boards. What to us was a huge scary surf pounding the shore, was to them a challenge to wring every bit of enjoyment out of. In retrospect, that cyclone was one of the most memorable events of our stay there and one we often talk about.

One thing we noticed in Mooloolaba for the first time and found in all the other places we stayed, was the friendliness of our host's neighbours and friends. Our second day there we received a phone call from their friends Ken and Kim up the hill in Buderim. They invited us to a barbecue the next evening and said they would pick us up.

On all of our exchanges we brought along little gifts for the people we would meet, as well as something special for the hosts. We tried to pick something local as well as lightweight. This time we brought a selection of BC and Canada calendars, both wall calendars and smaller desk size. The gift we left for our hosts was a locally made dreamcatcher to go over their bed. When Ken came to pick us up we had a couple of calendars with us as well as a hostess gift of a bottle of wine. As soon as we got in the car Ken told us to take note of the route we went as we would be driving ourselves the next time. It was nice to know we had a second invitation before we'd even started our first visit.

18

We were excited to be going to our first Aussie Barbie, and indeed shrimp was on the menu that night. Another first was a game of Bocce on their back lawn, played by moonlight.

One of the other guests at the barbecue was a lady named Mary who said she had an industrial kitchen in her house and made dressings, sauces and jams that she sold at the Eumundi Market. I had read about the Eumundi Market and said that it was on our list of places to go. However, as it was an hour's drive away on a busy highway, Doug wanted to get more practice driving on the left side of the road before he attempted it. Mary said that she was going to the market on Saturday (this was Thursday), and if I wanted to go with her, she'd love to have me, although I should know that she would pick me up at 5 am. It was a hour's drive, the market opened at 7 am, and she needed an hour to set up her booth before she opened for business. I was still waking up early because of jet lag so figured I could manage that. She also said it would be nice if I could look after her booth for a while during the day so she could walk around the market herself, as she seldom got a chance to do this. We agreed that I would go with her for the day, work in her booth and we would both have some time for personal shopping.

The next day, I realized that if I was going to be selling stuff, I needed to make change and I didn't know Aussie money that well. So, Doug and I emptied our pockets and laid out some cash. It is quite different from ours. The bills are multi-colored and have plastic inserts. The coins are different sizes from ours and different denominations. First, they have no pennies. Everything is priced ending in 5 or 0. The 5-cent piece, instead of being big like ours is very tiny, smaller than our dime. The 10-cent coin is bigger than ours but smaller and thinner than our nickel. They have no quarters, instead they have 20 cent pieces which are about the size of our quarter. They also have 50 cent pieces, which are larger than our quarter, and are a darker silver with a ridged edge. The $1.00 coin is large and copper colored. They have a $2.00 coin which is smaller than the $1.00, twice as thick and also a brown color. I memorized what they looked like and felt like, and practised making change of various amounts. It was a good practical exercise as I was always comfortable with the cash after that.

Mary picked me up on Saturday morning and during the drive to Eumundi she described her products, what they were made of and what they were used for. She had listed all the products and their prices on a note pad, so at least I didn't have to remember them.

I thoroughly enjoyed my day at Eumundi Market. We both worked the booth the first two hours after opening as that was very busy. Mary then suggested that I take a hour or so to walk around the market and see what was available, then make my last stop the coffee shop before returning. I did, adding a couple of cinnamon buns to go with the coffee. When we finished our mid-morning snack, Mary left to make her round of the market.

I sold quite a lot of Mary's products that day, not because of my knowledge of the products, but because people heard my accent and stopped to talk to me, then bought something while they were there. One encounter I initiated. I spotted an older man walking through the market wearing a ball cap with "McGill" on the front. I called out to him and asked,

"Is that McGill as in McGill University in Montreal?"

He came to an abrupt halt and said "How astute of you to notice that." He then went on to explain that his son was a professor at McGill and had sent the cap to him at Christmas. We chatted a bit and he bought some jam.

The market closed at 3 pm and as soon as it closed there was a rush of socializing and trading among the vendors. Mary traded a bottle of salad dressing for a loaf of bread from the vendor in the next booth, then put an assortment of her products in a bag and went for a walk. She returned with two huge shopping bags filled with vegetables and fruits that she'd traded for. She gave one of the bags to me, so I guess that was my pay for working her booth for the day.

While I was spending the day at Eumundi Market with Mary, Doug was golfing with Ken at his golf club, so we had separate but interesting days. A couple of weeks later we drove to Eumundi

Market ourselves, walked all around the market and made a few purchases.

One day we drove to the Australian Zoo for the day. This is the zoo owned by the late Steve Irwin and is still run by his family. In those days Steve and his family were quite "hands on" in running the zoo and we hoped to see them around the place. However, we were told that they were off on location filming their TV show. The zoo is quite a fascinating place

We wandered all over it, stopping to see a crocodile feeding, a show with employees playing with baby lions, a snake emporium, and finally, an enclosure where we could go in to see and pet tame kangaroos and wallabies. I even got to hold a Koala for a few minutes. But although the girl who passed him to me draped a blanket over my shoulder first, the Koala's fearsome claws still dug into me so I was happy to give him back.

When we were tired of walking there was a restaurant with lunch and snack foods. We had pineapple shells filled with chopped fruit and ice cream. They were more dessert than lunch, but absolutely delicious.

Another day we drove to the Big Pineapple, a working pineapple farm with a little train that wound through the fields with a guide doing a commentary and ending at –guess what? A gift shop and restaurant. It was at the Big Pineapple that I bought my largest souvenir purchase of the trip, a red leather Jillaroo hat. A Jackaroo is a Australian cowboy, and the female equivalent is called a Jillaroo, so I guess my purchase was basically a red leather cowboy hat. It was made by a well-known Australian manufacturer of hats and has the brand name burned into the leather inside the crown. It's by far the most expensive hat I've ever purchased and I love it. 14 years later, I'm still wearing it.

One of the things people seem to do a lot in Australia is go to coffee shops. There are coffee shops all over and the coffees are rather strange. It's difficult to find a good cup of North American coffee, except at McDonald's. The Aussie coffee shops don't seem to serve coffee in mugs, instead, the cold drinks are in tall glasses and the hot ones are in short wide cups. Something called Flat White is in a cup only about two inches high but almost as big around as the saucer. It's kind of a beige colored coffee with a brownish scum on the top. I found it totally unappetizing looking. I did like their mochas though. Most of the coffee shops are either out in the open or have sidewalk access from a patio, so they're a good place to sit and people watch.

We found people watching from the coffee shops rather interesting. Australia, because of the hot climate, is a bikini and bare skin culture. One morning we were amused to see a very pregnant woman walking by in a bikini. To add to it, or perhaps the reason she was wearing a bikini, was that she had a tattoo on her belly. We wondered if the tattoo got bigger as she did and when she had the baby if the tattoo would get small and wrinkled. It was probably completely normal for her, but it gave me something to write about in my weekly e-mail back home.

About our third week in Mooloolaba, we saw a tourist brochure about Fraser Island and it looked really interesting. We called and found out there was a tour bus leaving from the mall in two days, so booked it. The tour bus turned out to be a bulky four-wheel-drive bus that was built like a tank. It held 20 people. It took almost four hours to get to Fraser Island, driving partly on the highway and partly on the beach. We had to take two ferries, one across a river and another over to the Island. The beach we drove on was lined with campers for most of its distance and we had to dodge fishermen and kids.

Once we got onto Fraser Island, we had to drive on the beach for the first while. The island roads were mainly rutted with soft sand and vehicles were prone to get stuck and have to be hauled out. You absolutely have to have a 4WD to drive on Fraser Island. In fact, at one place where we drove off the beach and onto a regular road, someone was bogged down in the sand in the cut-through road. We had to stop and we got stuck as well. Everyone on the bus got off and helped push the first guy out, then pushed the bus. When we got off the ferry to the island, the bus driver was told he had 20 minutes to drive around the headland before the tide got too high. So he took off at high speed along the beach, dodging huge jelly fish (some of them two feet across) and bits of driftwood. There were two places where the driving space was quite narrow. One was around a headland with huge cliffs on one side and the ocean on the other. The tide was coming in and was actually touching the cliff in some places. Our driver had to time his driving to the waves. He never actually stopped the bus, but sort of zig-zagged. Later he told us that it would have been a disaster to stop, as the sand, when it gets wet, is somewhat like quicksand and the bus would have begun to sink within seconds.

The second narrow place was called Mud Rocks, and was the only place on the beach where there were rocks. Here we had to stay mostly outside the rocks and drive with our wheels in the water. In one place he drove over some low rocks. When we got to our next pit stop, there was a huge bulletin board outside the restrooms with photos of 4WDs and busses that waited too long to drive through Mud Rocks. Some were in water up to their roof. Others were upside down. But they were almost all badly battered from being rolled over and over by the waves and tossed up on the rocks.

And people use that beach like a highway every day!!! It boggles the mind.

We had lunch in a picnic area by a perched lake. This is a lake about 200 feet above sea level in a circular depression in the center of a sand dune. The sand is pure white and is composed mainly of silica. Much like the sand at White Sands, New Mexico. The driver suggested that if we were wearing any gold jewellery to go to the water's edge and rub it with a mixture of sand and water. Doug went in swimming and did rub his wedding ring with the wet sand. The driver was right, it really sparkled when he came out. Later that evening he also remarked how smooth the soles of his feet were. The silica was just like pumice and cleaned all the dead skin and calluses off. I walked in the sand as well, but just the dry sand, and it didn't scrub like the wet sand did.

On the way back, the tide was out and the beach was like a four-lane highway – about 200 yards wide and hard packed. As it was Sunday afternoon and all the locals, who were out for the day, were also on their way home on the last low tide of the day. The traffic was like a mainland highway, only without the lines.

While we were waiting for the ferry, the driver pointed out a couple of box jellyfish lying on the sand and said we could get out and look at it if we wished. But he warned us not, under any circumstance, to touch it, even with a stick. He said it was one of the most dangerous and venomous creatures in the sea. It could kill a grown person with its sting and even a dead one had enough toxin to make a person very sick.

A very interesting day.

The next day we went to a camera shop as I had dropped my camera in the sand while photographing the group pushing the bus. It was a Minolta SLR and even though I cleaned it off when I got back on the bus, it now made a grating noise when I turned the lens to focus it, and was getting increasingly stiffer to use. As soon as the camera store people heard that I had dropped it on Fraser Island, they shook their heads. They said the silica sand was so fine that, once it got into the internal works, it was impossible to get it all out and it would just wear away all the moving parts. We couldn't be without a camera on this trip, so a few days later, after shopping around, we bought a new one.

I brought the old one home though, on the off-chance it could be fixed. And someone eventually did. Some months later, our daughter had a computer problem and a tech support guy in the library where she works fixed it for her. He wouldn't take any payment for the job, so she gave him my old camera, saying that if he could fix computers maybe he could fix cameras as well. He took the camera completely apart, soaked all the parts in some kind of solvent, let it air dry for a few days and put it together again. It then worked perfectly and he was happy with his new camera and even fixed her computer for her again.

One thing North Americans will find different about Australia is the TV shows. On the surface, when you check the TV Guide, they look the same, but the shows themselves are totally different. Australian TV buys or leases the name and then does their own show. The first time we watched Wheel of Fortune there we were shocked. There was no Pat or Vanna. Instead, the host was a guy named Ned and the letter turner was a blonde who smiled when she was facing the audience or twitched her rear when turning the letters, but didn't say a word or interact with anyone during the show.

The first time we saw the Aussie version of Who Wants to be a Millionaire, Regis, impeccably dressed in a suit and tie, was still the host back home. Here a casually dressed host joked with the audience before getting on with the show. The easy questions were all about Australian TV shows and sports and we didn't know any of the answers. The harder questions were broader based and some of these we did know. Australian Survivor had an Aussie host and was set in a remote part of Australia. We also saw a trailer for a new show called Temptation Island and it was filled with topless girls and bare bums on the beach. We never did see an episode of that show, but didn't think it would pass the censors back home.

We saw our hosts' friends, Ken and Kim, several times during our stay in Mooloolaba. Doug golfed with Ken a few times and one day

Kim invited me to a luncheon meeting of her University Women's Club. I was introduced as "a guest from the other side of the world" and asked to say a few words. I told them all about home exchanging and how much we were enjoying our stay in Mooloolaba. We also invited Ken and Kim to dinner at our place one night to share our last pork roast. At that time, we were also negotiating our next exchange, which would be in the north of England, and found out that Ken and Kim would be in England at the same time, so we made arrangements to keep in touch and perhaps get together there.

We left Australia with many fond memories, some new friends, and the realization that we had found a new lifestyle; a new way to travel and were very much looking forward to the next exchange.

Chapter 4

OUR BRITISH RELATIVES

ALTHOUGH AUSTRALIA WAS FIRST on our list of preferred places to exchange, Britain was a close second.

Doug's mother was originally from the north of England, a town called Stockport just outside Manchester. She had been a war bride from the First World War. It was quite a romantic story, actually. Doug's father, Prescott, was a soldier in the Nova Scotia Highlanders. After training in Canada, he was shipped to Europe where he was wounded in the battle at Vimy Ridge. He was subsequently sent to England to recover from his injuries and ended up in a hospital in Manchester where Doug's mother, Louisa, was working as a nurse. The two clicked immediately and they were married in 1919 in Stockport shortly before Prescott was sent back to Canada. After the war, Louisa travelled to Canada on a ship full of other war brides, arriving at Halifax's Pier 21.

Over the years, Doug's mother, and later his two sisters, kept in touch with the British side of the family through frequent letters. His mother and sisters also visited England in the early 30s, before Doug was born. Today, we keep up the correspondence, although ours is through e-mail. At one time Doug had several first cousins in the Manchester area, but they are all gone now and the ones we keep in touch with are second cousins, the next generation.

We had first visited England back in the early 80s when our two teenagers were in Air Cadets and their squadron arranged an exchange trip to the Manchester area. We volunteered to go as escorts and chaperones as we knew we would have some free time there and would be able to visit the cousins. We stayed with Doug's first cousin, Arnold, in Stockport for a few days and then took the train to London for the remainder of our free time.

Our first night at Arnold's, he invited about 10 of the cousins and spouses to his house and we all went out to a restaurant for dinner. That was our first time meeting them face to face. We're not sure what kind of impression we made as we were having trouble staying awake the whole evening. The previous day we had finished our packing and arrived at the airport for our evening flight. We got no sleep on the plane as the cadets, in their teens, were all excited about the trip and they didn't sleep until a couple of hours before landing. We had to keep reminding them to be quiet as most of the other passengers wanted to sleep. The cadets were met by their exchange hosts and Arnold picked us up. He took us to his house first and then announced that he had a sightseeing trip planned for us. We spent all day driving around to places like Chester and Blackpool. I was in the back seat and managed a few short naps but Doug had to stay awake and talk to Arnold. Then back at his house, he announced that the other family members would be arriving within the hour if we would like to freshen up. We were definitely not fresh and we both desperately needed a nap as we hadn't slept since the previous morning. However, a quick face wash and a change of clothes was all we got. We spent the whole evening desperately trying to keep our eyes open. The next day neither of us could remember the names of anyone we'd met.

Many years had passed since our first visit, so another trip to England was on our list of things to do, while the older first cousins were still around. The problem now was who to stay with, as the older ones had downsized and the younger cousins all had growing families and most likely had little room for visitors. A home exchange in a central location, within an easy drive of most of them, seemed the perfect solution. It took us almost a year to find an exchange in the perfect location, but we eventually did. It was in the village of

Hartford, near Norwich, just 15 kilometers from Linda and Keith's house in Stockport.

Our hosts this time were Jim and Jeanine, both teachers. The exchange was in August as they had to be back home for their September school opening. Jim was a retired football (soccer to us) player who taught physical education at the local high school and was also their sports coach. They had a married daughter who lived nearby and a son still living at home. The son was staying with friends while we were there, but came by a few times to pick up mail and things he needed but forgot to take with him.

Here we encountered another electrical appliance that didn't work in a way we were used to. The first time I did laundry it worked fine. Then the second time the clothes came out of the dryer still damp. Putting them in for a second time didn't help, they were still damp but also very hot. Thinking the lint trap was full, I searched the machine for it and discovered that it had no vent. I noticed a drawer on one side of the dryer and, thinking it was the lint trap, pulled it out. To my surprise, the drawer was filled with hot water, which went flying everywhere when I yanked it open. We realized then that, as the dryer had no vent, all the water from the wet clothes was collected in this drawer and it had to be emptied after every load for the clothes to dry. Once we figured that out the clothes dried OK.

Hartford was a great central place for us to stay. We could visit the relatives and socialize with them individually, or in a group, as when cousin Valerie invited everyone to her house for a brunch. Or we could invite them to our place for dinner, which we did. Being on our own with no obligation to a host or hostess meant that we could spend a lot of our time sightseeing.

The car we got to drive on this exchange was a sporty looking Mini Cooper. Doug, at six feet three inches, had a problem getting into this car. It was accomplished only by arranging his legs and arms in a sequence. Once in, there was plenty of room, so it was an easy fit that way. He claimed that he didn't get into this car, he wore it. The Mini Cooper had a stick shift with five gears on the floor which had to be shifted with the left hand, so that took some getting used to.

Once we were comfortable with the car, we drove all over the north of England and even into Wales. One of our favorite trips was to Carnarvon Castle in Wales.

On our trip to Carnarvon, we took an interesting side trip that involved Doug's family history. His mother had often talked about the "holiday fortnight" that her family took every summer in Wales when she was a child. They always rented the same house, and obviously she had fond memories of her visits there. Doug's sister, Marjorie, had her mother's old photo album and in it was a photograph taken from the front porch of this vacation house. She gave us the photo when we told her that Wales was one of the places we planned to go. It was a photo of a bay with some sailboats and an odd shaped headland on one side. We decided to see if we could find it and take another photo from the same location. We knew the houses and the shore would be different after so many years, but thought we could find it from the shape of the bay and headland.

To our surprise, we did find it. The odd shaped headland looked exactly the same. Unfortunately, nothing else was the same and when we finally lined up the photo with what we were seeing, we were standing in the middle of a parking lot between a petrol (gas) station and a line of stores that we would refer to as a strip mall. Absolutely nothing remained of the row of vacation cottages that she remembered so fondly. We're rather glad that Doug's mother never saw it as it is. Sometimes memories are better than the reality.

We had kept in touch with Ken and Kim from Australia and knew they would be in the town of Chester on a certain date. Chester is about 40 miles from Hartford, where we were staying, so we made arrangements to meet them at a certain pub, just off the main square, for dinner. It was great getting together again and discussing our trips. The owner of the pub, when he realized we were from two different countries on the other side of the world meeting for dinner at his place, insisted on taking our picture with his bar in the background to hang on the wall with his celebrity guest photos. It would be interesting to know if it's still there.

Over the years, one of our tactics for cutting travel costs has been to maximize our air flights. That is, to do two or more trips, activities or destinations utilizing one long flight. On this exchange to Britain, we included two add-ons. One was a Brit-Rail pass and the other was a coach tour of Scotland.

Our Brit-Rail passes were senior eight-trip passes. Brit-Rail passes, if bought before you leave your home country, are quite inexpensive compared to single tickets bought within Britain. Senior passes gave us another 25% off. Each trip on the pass is actually more than a trip; it is as far as you can travel in one 24-hour period. Our trip to London was two trips on the pass as we stayed for several days before returning. On the other hand, our trips to Portsmouth from London and to Liverpool from Hartford used up only one trip each as we returned the same day. We also used our passes to get to Edinburgh for the start of our coach tour and to return to Manchester from Glasgow at the end of the tour. We had intended to stay three days in Glasgow, but our coach tour included a city tour and there really wasn't much more to see. We knew we still had two trips left on our rail passes and we needed only one to get back to Manchester to catch our flight home. After checking a rail map for possibilities, we decided to go to Aberdeen for the day. It was a four-hour train trip, so we left early in the morning, had lunch in Aberdeen and walked around the downtown, then caught the afternoon train back to Glasgow. We both love trains, so spending the day on a train, watching the scenery go by, dozing and reading, was a treat for us. Then the next day we used our last rail passes to go back to Manchester for our flight home.

Our coach tour of Scotland was memorable for several reasons. One was that it included the famous Edinburgh Tattoo at Edinburgh Castle. Our enjoyment of this was rather mixed. Although we were awed by the grandeur of the castle grounds, the music and the marching, and the breath-catching sound of the Lone Piper at the top of the castle that ended the show, it was all marred by the rain. Not just a Scotch Mist that they seem to have a lot but a real downpour. Entrepreneurs by the roadside on the way to the castle were selling plastic ponchos, but they didn't cover much, and by the time we got to the grandstands they were soaked as well, and uncomfortable to sit on. Even though we were soaked and miserable, the performers must have been more so with their huge heavy bearskin hats and dripping wool kilts. So although the show and location were magnificent, most of the audience was happy to head back to their hotels for hot showers and dry clothes.

A quest for a tartan also didn't turn out quite as I expected. My mother's family name is Elliott, which is a Scottish border clan. I thought it would be nice to purchase a couple of yards of the Elliott tartan to make a skirt, and what better place to get it than from the source? I told our tour guide about my wish to visit a tartan shop and he said we would actually be visiting several along the way. The first two we visited had no Elliott tartan fabric, only small souvenirs such as coffee mugs and key chains. The tartan on these was too small to see what the tartan actually looked like. In a shop in Inverness in the north of Scotland when I asked a clerk about the Elliott tartan, he said he thought they might have some "down cellar". I followed him down three flights of stairs that got progressively narrower, into what seemed like the bowels of the earth, and which smelled mustier with each flight. At the bottom he opened a heavy squeaky door into a room lined with shelves that were piled high with rolls of fabric. After poking around for a few minutes, he pulled out one and unrolled it with a flourish across a cutting table in the center of the room. I stared at it for a moment and then said the first thing that came to mind, "That is the ugliest tartan I have ever seen."

"Well," he said, "We don't have much call for it these days." I climbed back up the stairs into the light and fresh air and informed the clerk that I would not be purchasing any tartan today. Alas, my quest for my mother's tartan had ended. I purchased a key chain and a notebook in the Elliott tartan. That small it didn't look too bad.

One stop on the tour didn't mean much to me but got Doug quite excited. It was at the famous St. Andrews Golf Course, the place where golf allegedly started. It was raining, as it did for most of this trip, but people were out on the course playing. When I commented on this, the tour escort said that most of those people had booked their tee times a year in advance. Many of them had travelled from other countries just to play this course. When the first tee was vacant momentarily, I took a quick photo of Doug standing there and then another next to the entrance sign. Then we went to the coffee shop to warm up and dry off a bit before getting back on the bus.

Another memorable stop on that coach tour was at Loch Ness, the home of the legendary lake monster, Nessie. We live in BC's Okanagan Valley and our Lake Okanagan has its own legendary monster, Ogopogo. We were interested to visit Loch Ness and see for ourselves if Nessie was as elusive as our Ogopogo. He was.

We got to see our cousins, Linda and Keith, once more. We had taken only one of our suitcases on the bus trip and left the other with them. They met us at the Manchester airport with our extra suitcase and had dinner with us before we boarded the plane for our trip home.

We left Britain with the feeling that we had done so much more than just a home exchange. We had travelled all over England and Wales on our own. We had visited with relatives that we kept in touch with but didn't see very often. We had toured Scotland and experienced the famous Edinburgh Castle Tattoo. But in the end, it was the home exchange that gave us a home base to make it all possible.

Chapter 5

A TRIPLE EXCHANGE

THE SUMMER OF 2005 and the winter of 2006 was our busiest travel year so far. That summer we completed another bucket list item, to drive across Canada coast to coast and back again. We decided to do it the proper way, travelling the whole distance on the Trans Canada Highway, from Mile 0 in Victoria, British Columbia, to Mile 0 in St. John's, Newfoundland, a trip of 7,714 kilometers or 4,628 miles. It's interesting that neither city wanted to be at the end of the highway, so both have Mile 0 markers. From the Maritime Provinces we drove south and then crossed the USA from coast to coast, visiting places such as Branson, Missouri, Pike's Peak and Yellowstone National Park.

This trip was connected, in a way, to our first multiple exchange trip to Australia the following winter. The exchange took almost a year to arrange as it had so many segments to it. We were still corresponding with people and making arrangements as we were travelling across the country, picking up e-mail at motels and at friends' houses while visiting. And for the first time, we were involved in a non-simultaneous exchange.

The first segment of the '06 Australian exchange that we finalized arrangements for was a vacation condo at Magic Mountain, near Surfer's Paradise on Queensland's Gold Coast. Although this was the first exchange we finalized, it was actually the third exchange in the list as it was scheduled for March. The owners, Lyle and Val, lived in Ballarat, near Melbourne, and went to the Gold Coast only in Australia's winter. They informed us they were not skiers, didn't like the cold, and preferred to come to Canada in our summer. People with vacation homes often do non-simultaneous exchanges, but we usually can't as we have only the one house. However, this summer our home would be empty while we were on our cross-country trip, so we were happy to tell them they could come while we were away. They arrived two days before we left on our road trip and we enjoyed a delightful visit with two lovely people. They have become our friends and we have since met up with them a couple of times. Once we met them in Stockholm, Sweden when we were on a Baltic cruise and they were doing an exchange. And two years later, on an exchange to Melbourne, we went to Ballarat and stayed with them for a few days. We still correspond with them a few times a year on email and with Christmas letters.

This trip also included our only problem with an exchange, which distressed us at first, but later became such a positive experience that we're glad it happened. We had arranged an exchange with a couple who had a condo in the downtown area of Sydney, near Darling Harbour. They were skiers and wanted to spend Christmas in Canada. At first we didn't want to be away at Christmas, then thought…why not? Christmas with access to a beach sounds pretty nice. This was all arranged early in the summer and we touched base about once a month. By November we were discussing making reservations for Christmas dinner for each other. Then we got a shocker e-mail. The Sydney couple, with the first and longest exchange, December 20 to January 25, advised us they were cancelling as they were getting divorced. We were shocked, and a little angry, as we felt that with such a momentous decision, they had to have some idea of it happening long before they told us. So here we were, only three weeks before departure, with a non-refundable airfare and no place to stay.

When we contacted Homelink, they in turn contacted their Australian agent, Lisa, and in the next week we got over a dozen e-mails from Aussie members. None of them wanted to exchange at that time, but the e-mails read like this: "If you don't find a place, we have a spare bedroom…" "We have an empty suite on our lower level…" or "We have a vacation home up the coast that we're not using right now…" We couldn't believe that so many people we didn't know were willing to help us, but as we got to know other members that we met we realized what great people they are.

We eventually found an exchange for most of that period on our own, not in Sydney, but in Brisbane. Doug and Terry, a couple living in a suburb of Brisbane had just joined Homelink and were excited about spending Christmas in Canada. However, they were both still working and could only come for three weeks. That left us with 10 days before the next exchange started, so we decided to spend it in Sydney anyway, as it's a city that we both love and enjoy.

The second exchange of that trip was in Burleigh Heads, a condo on the beach on the Gold Coast, quite close to Magic Mountain our third exchange, which was Lyle and Val's place. So now, three weeks before Christmas and two weeks before departure, we finally had all arrangements made. Whew!

My biggest problem now was how to pack for three months. I was never one to travel light and I also love to shop in new locations. What kicked in now was a trick I've used on other occasions. I chose a couple of good outfits to wear when socializing, then packed mainly my oldest clothes and rattiest underwear, planning to ditch them along the way as I acquired new things. A pair of walking shoes, well worn and well scuffed, didn't come home either.

Doug and Terry arrived the day before we left. We told them we'd be wearing red Santa hats so they could find us in the airport. They got off the plane also wearing Santa hats, so we found each other easily. We were able to show them how things worked in the house, then took them on a quick tour of the neighborhood, pointing out the supermarket, pharmacy and the nearest coffee shop. The next morning, we toured our clubhouse, which they were welcome to use as guests, and introduced them to several of our neighbors, then we took them to visit the nearest winery. It snowed that morning so Doug (the Aussie Doug) got a lesson in snow shovelling and driving in the snow. Later that afternoon they drove us to the airport for our flight to Vancouver to start our adventure.

This trip we decided to go a totally different way. We had never been to Asia so flew to Australia via Hong Kong with a plan to stay in Hong Kong for a few days on the return trip. We had booked this flight through Air Canada but opted to fly on their partner airline Cathay Pacific which is based in Hong Kong. Crossing the International Date Line between Vancouver and Hong Kong meant that we lost a day. We left home on December 20 and arrived in Hong Kong 12 hours later on the 22nd. December 21st never happened.

Flying Cathay Pacific was an interesting experience. The flight attendants were all young women, some of whom looked like they were still in their teens, and they ran constantly. Serving meals, they ran down the aisle with stacks of trays, they ran back and forth replenishing the drinks cart. They wore rubber soled shoes so you couldn't hear them coming. We almost came to grief with them a few times. Once I woke up with a cramp in my leg and stuck the foot out in the aisle to work the cramp out just as one ran by. She momentarily tripped over my foot, then leaped over it and kept going. Getting up to go to the bathroom almost resulted in another collision. Even sticking my head out in the aisle to see if anyone was coming before getting up was hazardous. I had to pull back fast as one zipped by. They never stopped and they were always feeding us. Hardly an hour went by, even in the middle of the night, without a drink or a snack being offered. Some of the snacks were quite different and quite delicious. Once they brought around pork buns. These were hot sweet buns with seasoned pork inside. Somewhat like a hot jelly donut with shredded pork instead of jelly buried in the middle. Flying is never fun, but we actually enjoyed flying Cathay Pacific and agreed we would do it again.

Terry's sister and her husband were at the Brisbane airport to meet us and took us to the house where we were to spend the next three weeks. They also invited us to a Christmas Eve barbecue at their house. The house we were staying in was on a residential street and had a pool in the backyard. As the temperature outside was 38C

(100F) the pool was one of the first things we enjoyed that day and almost every day we were there.

On Christmas Eve, December 24, we phoned our son Pete to say Happy Birthday. His birthday is the 23rd, but because of the time difference it was still the 23rd back in Canada when we called.

We have often commented that Australia has the friendliest people in the world and the most unfriendly critters. Topping the list of unfriendly critters are sharks, crocodiles and snakes, but luckily, we never encountered any of those on a personal basis. Friendly people, however, we encountered everywhere we went. And Christmas Eve in Brisbane was just the beginning. Early in the morning a neighbour, Reg, from across the street came over to show us how to clean the pool filter. This was a job we'd agreed to do, a small enough price for the use of a private pool throughout our stay. He stayed for a chat and ended up inviting us to a party at the end of the street in the afternoon. We were treated to an example of Aussie humor. He told us the party was in the front yard of two ladies, one of whom was named Denise. He couldn't remember the name of the other because he always called them Denise and Denephew. At the party we found out the other lady was named Robin. There were twelve houses on the street and it seemed that everyone was there at the get-together, and they all knew who we were. So obviously we, and the reason we were there, were objects of curiosity.

We had to leave the street party early as we were expected at Terry's sister Tracy's house for dinner, and we had our first long drive to get there. That evening we participated in a typical Aussie dinner party, eating outside on the deck with food cooked on the Barbie. One of the interesting people we met that night was a marathon runner whose son came third in his age group (18-24) in the Hawaii Ironman. He was interested to know that we lived close to Penticton BC, as his son wanted to use the Penticton Ironman the next summer as his qualifier for the next winter's Hawaii Ironman race, and he and his wife planned to travel to Penticton to see him run. We told them that we had seen the race two years previously when our son's girlfriend had run it, and we gave them our card and invited them to call us when they arrived in Penticton, as it is an easy drive from our home.

Getting back home later that night was not as easy as getting to the party. We took a wrong turn in the dark and got completely lost. We stopped at a service station to read the map and discovered we were heading out of town. We asked directions and marked our map. Heading off again we were on the right highway but overshot our exit and ended up by the Port of Brisbane. We turned around and headed back the way we thought was right, but we weren't sure. We pulled into a shopping center parking lot to read the map again and discovered we were in the same shopping center where we'd grocery shopped earlier in the day. We knew our way home from there, so more by good luck then good management we made it back to the house. It was not very comfortable being lost in the dark in a city we didn't know. In those days we didn't own a GPS. Today it would be much easier.

As for the unfriendly critter encounter – earlier in the day I was held hostage by a hoard of ants. I was sitting out on the patio reading when I felt a tickling sensation on one foot, looked down and saw ants running across my bare foot. I brushed them off, propped my feet on another chair and went on reading. A short time later Doug called to me and I couldn't go in the house as the patio was covered in ants and I yelled to him that I was being held hostage. He came out with a broom and cleared a path so I could run to the back door. I made sure I had no ants on me before going into the house.

Christmas Day in Australia is certainly different from Christmas Day back home. Aussies mainly go to the beach and barbecue their dinner on one of the many public barbecues in the parks lining the beaches. We planned to do the same until we found out that most people go about 5:30 in the morning to stake out their favorite spot, carrying with them everything they'll need for the day. Since parking on that day is at a premium, late comers have to park a long distance away wheeling their coolers and beach chairs on wagons or strollers, or making several trips. Since we didn't have any of those things, and we didn't think our white, untanned skin could stand several hours on a beach in the sun, we opted to be sensible and eat dinner at home. We decided we would eat an Aussie style lunch and purchased two pounds of jumbo prawns. Unlike at home, however, these guys still had their heads and shells on, so we had to work for our lunch. For Christmas dinner we had cold take-out chook and salad. Chook is Aussie for chicken. We spent the afternoon in the pool, as we did most afternoons that we weren't out sightseeing.

The day after Christmas, knowing it was still Christmas Day back home, we called our daughter, Kristal, to wish her a Merry Christmas. Then we went to the mall. Over the next few weeks, we spent a lot of time at one of the nearby malls, not so much to shop as to walk in air-conditioned comfort, as it was so hot outside. I never thought I'd complain about the heat, but the Australian sun was too much for even a heat lover like me.

We found Brisbane to be a very challenging city to drive in, and as we already found driving on the left a bit difficult, we didn't want to add to the stress level, so we used city transit as much as possible. We really liked the ferry system. There was a ferry dock with a large parking lot only a short drive from our house, so it was convenient for us. From there a quick ferry ride took us to the downtown area where we could walk on Queen Street. Queen Street is a car-free pedestrian street, about eight blocks long, lined with stores, restaurants and coffee shops, with a casino at one end. Once we were at the Queen Street dock, we could get the fast ferry called the City-Cat. The City-Cat followed the river from one end of the city to the other. One day we stayed on it for the complete round trip which took almost two hours.

The river is the reason Brisbane is so difficult to drive. It snakes through the city, curving back on itself. There are some straight streets, while others curve to follow the river, then others go diagonally between the two. A street that crosses the river has a different name on the other side and usually doesn't line up anyway. Since downtown Queen Street is a no-traffic pedestrian mall it effectively stops traffic in the cross streets, most of which are one-way. There is absolutely no grid system as most city downtown areas have. In most cities the north/south streets cross the east/west streets. In Brisbane most of the main streets are diagonal and when they reach the river they change direction, and usually change names. I always considered myself a good map reader, but Brisbane completely baffled me. The bus system, however, is quite straightforward. You get on a bus in the suburbs and it takes you downtown. You make a note of the name of the stop and the bus number and take the same one home. The ferry system on the river works much the same way. Once we figured that out, we travelled all over the city with no problem.

New Year's in Australia was as different as Christmas. Not wanting to get caught up in New Year's Eve traffic, we had dinner in a restaurant about a three block walk from our house. The restaurant was Chinese and had some of the best Chinese food we've ever had. We have always enjoyed the Chinese food in Australia. It's far better than back home, perhaps because it's more authentic. At 9 pm the plaza where the restaurant was located did a fireworks show. It was just a small one, but good. Back home at midnight we watched the fireworks display on the Sydney Bridge on TV. Now THAT was fireworks.

Another difference was the names of the stores. Australia is very much "Australia First" and most stores are local. They just don't have the big chain department stores that we are used to in Canada or the USA. The two largest grocery chains are Coles and Woolworths, which we knew back home in a different context. Coles in Canada is a book store, and Woolworths used to be a downscale department store before Walmart bought it out. We've bought food here in Price-Freezer, a store that sells only frozen food, mostly packed in portion sizes, much like our M & M stores. We've also shopped in a store called Crazy's that sells the kind of stuff we would buy back home in a Dollar store or Walmart. The clothing stores in the malls mostly are named for the owners, so you have to go in and look to see what it is they sell. My favorite was one called Miller's. They seemed to have the kind of clothes I wear and in my sizes. They are excellent quality as well. Years after first shopping in their stores, I'm still wearing the clothes I bought there.

One thing Australia didn't have when we were travelling there was factory outlets. They had a couple of stores with that name attached and an actual factory outlet mall in one city we were in, but using the name didn't mean they actually were outlets. In Canada and the USA factory outlets start at 50% off and go from there. In the Aussie version the signs read: "reg $39 ea, now 2 for $70", or "massive reductions, 20% off". In my opinion, when we're talking factory outlets, 20% off just doesn't cut it.

The only time I ever actually got a bargain on clothes in Australia was one day at Miller's in a mall. They had a sale rack tucked in the back with a small sign "everything on sale $10." Most of the stuff was odds and ends that they couldn't sell for regular price, such as tops or bottoms missing the other half. But then I pulled out a pair of stretch jeans that were marked two sizes smaller than I would usually wear. They looked like they would fit, and they did. So, I got a pair of mis-sized jeans for $10, and years later I'm still wearing them. The big difference between there and here is that here at home that sale rack would be right up front instead of hidden in the back almost out of sight.

Our second exchange on this trip was a condo in Burleigh Heads on the Gold Coast, about 50 miles south of Brisbane. It was a vacation home owned by Bill and Jackie, who lived in Brisbane. Since they were right there in the city, we called to say hello and talk about getting keys, etc. They invited us to visit, so we did. We got a tour of their beautiful home and also of Bill's collection of automotive memorabilia.

As our exchange at their place didn't start until February 1st and we were leaving our Brisbane exchange two weeks before that, we looked at several options. What we eventually did was take the train from Brisbane to Sydney, stopping for three days in Coff's Harbour, which is about halfway. We booked a condo in Darling Harbour, a Sydney suburb, for a week, then a flight to Adelaide, where we stayed for four days, then another flight from Adelaide back to Brisbane. You might wonder why we spent all that money on flights when we could have just stayed in one place for the two weeks. Well, we learned early on that flying is very cheap in Australia. With Australia being such a large country and most of it empty wilderness, flying is the most efficient way to get anywhere, and also the cheapest. Although Qantas is the national airline and does most of the overseas flights, Virgin Blue is king of the short haul flights with deep discounts. In addition, they have half-price flights before 8 am and after 8 pm. So, especially if you time your flights right, flying beats trains, busses or driving in price as well as time.

When we gave Bill and Jackie our itinerary, Bill asked for our flight number and arrival time and said he would pick us up at the airport and drive us back to his place to get the car we would drive during the month we would be at their place in Burleigh Heads. That was when we found out that they had a change of plans. Our previous arrangement was that they would stay at our place for the first two weeks in February and then go to visit friends in Los Angeles. The friend in LA was also a car buff, and at the last minute he was able to obtain two tickets to the Daytona 500 race in Daytona, Florida. Given the choice of spending two weeks in snowy Kelowna or two weeks in sunny Florida, Daytona won out. We expect Jackie was happier with this arrangement as Bill was the skier who wanted to ski at Big White and Jackie didn't ski. They were no longer planning on a trip to Kelowna. We said we would "bank" the exchange owing and they could come sometime when we were travelling elsewhere. Although we kept in touch for many years, they never did come.

When Doug and Terry arrived back home, we picked them up at the airport and then they drove us to the train station. Australia has a great train system and we used it often in our various trips there. This route from Brisbane to Sydney was right down the coast and in some places had a view of the ocean from the train. Since it was strictly a day passenger train, not a sleeper, there was no dining car. But they did have a lounge car with a bar that sold sandwiches and drinks that you could take back to your seat. We also had some cheese and cookies with us. We knew the place we'd rented in Coff's

Harbour had a kitchen so had brought a large tote bag with some essentials in it.

Our first night there, however, we spotted a seafood restaurant nearby so went there for one of the most unusual and delicious meals we've ever had. Doug had a dish called Bongo-Bongo which turned out to be jumbo prawns wrapped in bacon, threaded on a kabob with chunks of banana, basted in soy sauce, grilled and served on a bed of jasmine rice. I had Moreton Bay Bugs and calamari served with pizza bread. The Bugs are a delicacy here. They look somewhat like elongated crabs and taste somewhat like lobster, but are much smaller, about 3 to 4 inches long.

Actually, Coff's Harbour turned out to be a bust. Their biggest attraction, The Big Banana, which is a working banana plantation turned theme park, was closed for renovations except for the gift shop. We mainly sat by the pool and read.

Our hotel in Darling Harbour, The Goldsborough, was very different. It used to be a wool storage warehouse, so its location, right on the harbour, was perfect. Because of its previous use, it had 14 foot ceilings in the rooms and 12 inch wide open beams in the public areas. The whole center of the building was hollow and from the lobby you could see the roof six floors above. Each floor had a walkway going all the way around the building, with wide plank flooring. The apartments were all accessed from this walkway. There were wide staircases, but also elevators. We had what's known as a self-catering suite, a one-bedroom apartment with a separate living room and kitchen. The second floor of the hotel had a walkway with access to the monorail to downtown, and just across the street was a complex that included a market, the Imax, the Maritime Museum and the Aquarium. In the distance we could see the tall buildings of downtown Sydney and the Sydney Tower. At night they were all lit up, so the view from our window was fabulous. Best of all, it was a short walk to the ferry dock, which was the easiest way to get downtown.

Our second day there we decided to visit the Queen Victoria Building in downtown Sydney. The QVB is advertised as the most beautiful shopping center in the world, and we have to agree. It's over 100 years old as it was built while old Vicky was still alive. Its different levels can be reached by a grand curving staircase and the staircase landings have huge stained-glass windows to the outside. In recent years they have installed escalators at the ends of the building, but you have to walk the staircases to appreciate the full splendour of the building.

When we were there, Sydney had a transit pass that you could buy for specific modes of transit, such as the subway, bus, monorail, or ferry system. Or you could buy one pass that covered all transit, as well as the Explorer Bus, which is a Hop-On, Hop-Off bus that goes to all the city attractions. The all-transit pass was expensive as it was marketed mainly to tourists, but worth it if you wanted to see everything. It was especially useful to us, staying in Darling Harbour, as we used the ferries to get to downtown, so we bought two one-week passes.

One day we spent most of the day on the Explorer Bus, visiting all the attractions. We walked around Circular Quay in the downtown area, visited the Art Gallery and then took the bus out to Bondi Beach. We walked along the beach boardwalk for a while watching the surfers, then went to a restaurant for an early dinner before heading back. Their daily special was Fish & Chips so we tried it but were mightily disappointed. It was the fishiest tasting fish I can ever remember eating. We asked what species of fish it was and were told flathead, a species of catfish. We'd eaten catfish in Florida and it was delicious so I suspect it was old and served to obvious tourists, who were not likely to return. Whatever the reason, we will never knowingly order flathead again!

Another day we went to tour the famed Sydney Opera House, but didn't get to see the inside. The tour involved climbing about 200 steps and neither of us felt we could do this without damage to our knees. We later saw a story in the newspaper about the Opera House being in bad shape and in need of extensive renovations. It was 50 years old with antiquated air conditioning, the roof was in bad shape with tiles regularly falling off, the stage and backstage were not big enough for contemporary touring companies, and the complex was not handicapped accessible. It had no escalators and only one small lift, as we found out when we were faced with the 200 steps. The government had pledged $70 million, but the architects were talking closer to $700 million. The newspaper headline read, "The Opera House is a world treasure, but we're stuck with the bill." Several years after that visit we were in Sydney again and the Opera House looked much better, so they must have found the money somewhere.

While we were in Sydney, we found out that we were to have a visit with my brother, Keith, and his wife Ann. They were touring Australia and going to visit friends who lived north of Brisbane. They had a few free days before meeting their friends, and when we told them we planned to go to Adelaide for four days, they opted to go there with us, so we changed our one-bedroom apartment rental in Adelaide to a two bedroom. It was a sister hotel to the Goldsborough called the Oakwood, and was the same type of place with self-catering apartments.

Keith and Ann were to arrive the day before we left for Adelaide and had planned to stay at an airport hotel that night as we were all flying to Adelaide the next day. A few days before their arrival we got an e-mail asking if we knew of a cheaper place to stay as they were shocked at the airport hotel's price. When we had checked into our hotel there was a note on the desk informing us that extra guests were $20 for rental of bedding and pillows for the sofa-bed in our living room. When we offered it to him, he gratefully accepted the cheaper digs. He liked $20 for the night better than the alternative. They arrived early in the morning after an overnight flight. As they had slept on the flight they were rested and ready to go, so we spent the day sightseeing. We ended the day at a type of restaurant that we had visited many times but was a novelty to them – an Aussie BBQ restaurant. This is a restaurant where you choose your steak from a refrigerated display case and cook it yourself on a huge barbecue. Then you choose the rest of the meal from a salad bar and a steam table of hot veggies. The price of the steak also includes fruit, rolls and coffee.

The next day, our last day in Sydney, was a holiday, January 26, Australia Day. This was comparable to our July 1, Canada Day or the USA's July 4, Independence Day. We had to check out of our hotel by 10 am, so we put our bags in storage at the hotel and spent the day taking in the celebrations around Darling Harbour. There was music, entertainment and food. We had Aussie Pies and beer for lunch, then caught the shuttle to the airport for our late afternoon flight to Adelaide.

We were very happy with our accommodations in Adelaide. The two-bedroom apartment had queen beds, each with its own bathroom, a living room, dining room and kitchen. There was also a terrace around two sides of the building, with a table and chairs on it. We picked up a pizza for dinner and ate it on the terrace watching the sunset with glasses of wine in hand. It doesn't get any better than this.

The next day we went looking for the Free Bus. There are two bus loops going through the downtown area and both are free. As far as we're concerned Free is Good.

That afternoon, as the guys were napping, Ann and I wandered through a nearby mall and went into an opal shop that had a re-creation of an opal mine in the basement. The owner obviously wasn't busy as he collared Ann and me and we got a half-hour lesson on opals, probably more than we wanted or needed to know, Certainly the opals he showed us were more than we could afford.

One day we did something we'd all been looking forward to, a full day tour of the Barossa Valley, Australia's major winemaking area. All four of us are wine buffs, Doug and I because we live in the Okanagan, BC's wine country, and Keith and Ann because they've traveled through Italy's and Germany's wine regions, sipping as they went.

The tour included four wineries as well as several other stops. The first stop was a wooden toy maker. Our brother Ed, who does woodworking, would have loved it, but we weren't interested, so we had a coffee and muffin in their coffee shop. The first winery we went to was a name we were familiar with, Wolf Blass. The wines we tasted, however, were just so-so, but their port was excellent, so we each bought a bottle.

The lunch stop featured Australian cuisine, so we all tried kangaroo steak with peppercorn sauce - no better time to try something different than on an Aussie wine tour. We all loved it. Ann said it had a faint taste of rabbit, so maybe that's why we enjoyed it. We all grew up eating rabbit as children, so it was familiar to us. Then we wondered if kangaroos and rabbits were a related species, as they both have powerful long back legs and hop using the back legs as a springboard, which made for a fun lunch discussion. The second winery wasn't very interesting so we didn't get anything. At the third winery the people were knowledgeable and their wines were OK, but nothing special. Some people on the bus bought some, but we didn't.

The last winery was the best of the lot. We enjoyed the wines and the people. Their Riesling was excellent. We tried a couple of ports and a white Muscat. One port we liked very much was called Bastardo. When questioned about the name, the girl behind the tasting bar said it was made from grapes from 200-year-old vines that no one knew the origin of, thus the grapes had no parentage and were bastards. This port also came in special hand painted bottles with sayings written on them. The one we bought read "Old Farts in Caravan Parks." As we are RVers, that was appropriate. Another read "Grumpy Old Men". They also had a very expensive port called The Forgotten Port. The story there was that the winery had changed hands a few years ago and one barrel was forgotten and unlabelled in the warehouse. They estimated it to be at least 40-year-old port, and those that tasted it said it was superb. Except for the Bastardo, which we enjoyed over the next few weeks, the best thing about this last winery was the entertainment. They regaled us with stories and we're not sure which, if any, were actually true.

Late that afternoon after the wine tour we had a silly session, playing in the water like kids. Perhaps we'd imbibed a little more wine than we thought. We were sitting out on the terrace enjoying

Happy Hour when Ann decided to do some stretches as she was stiff from sitting in the bus all day. I commented on how dirty the bottoms of her feet were. Then I looked at mine and they were just as dirty. We'd been walking on the terrace in our bare feet and it was probably covered in soot from the wildfires still burning just outside Adelaide. As we had a Jacuzzi tub in one of our bathrooms, we went in, ran water in it and sat on the edge of the tub. We didn't get much suds from the shower gel we put in, so dumped in some shampoo and turned on the jets. Within minutes we had bubbles coming up the sides of the tub. We got bubbles on ourselves and started laughing. Doug and Keith heard the laughing, came in, took off their shoes and climbed in as well. The four of us were sitting on the edge of the tub, splashing in the water, playing footsie, soaking ourselves, throwing suds and behaving like five-year-olds. But we did come out with clean feet.

Adelaide has a transportation system that we have never seen anywhere else. The city is very spread out with suburbs a long way from down town. We wanted to go to a shopping center that was a long way out and it was recommended that we take the O-Bahn. In the city the bus looks just like any other bus. The only difference is that it has small sideways wheels just in front of the front wheels. Once outside the downtown it drives onto a dedicated track, sliding the front sideways wheels into a groove in the track, much like a train merging onto a main track. Then it accelerates to 120km. WOW! We were then zipping through parkland and backyards with only two stops in 20km. At the end of the line, the shopping center, with its own parking lot, was on one side of the track, and a huge multi-level parking garage was on the other side. Obviously, this was a popular way to commute into the city. We're amazed we haven't seen this before. It certainly is more cost-effective than digging subways or building elevated monorails. The whole track bed, with a track in each direction, was barely wider than two buses, so it wouldn't take up more room than a narrow city street. It was fenced, of course, to keep people and animals off the tracks.

The next day we left Adelaide and started on our next exchange in Burleigh Heads. All four of us flew together to Brisbane where Doug and I were picked up at the airport, as planned, by Bill. Keith and Ann flew on to Cairns where they planned to meet up with friends they had met previously on a coach tour through Italy.

Bill drove us back to his house in Brisbane where Jackie was busy packing for their US trip. He had previously asked us which car we wanted and we said whatever had automatic drive, as Doug found that driving on the left and managing a stick shift was uncomfortable. What he had for us was a Holden Ute or pickup truck. There was a snap-on cover over the truck box, or tray as they called it, so we loaded our luggage in there. Jackie gave us a box of fruit, vegetables and other perishable items from their fridge that they couldn't use as they were leaving the next day. We got a map and directions and set off down the Pacific Highway. Burleigh Heads was not very far, only an hour's drive.

We knew the condo building was tall as we'd been told our exchange condo was a 25th floor sub-penthouse. What we didn't know was that it was the tallest building around. It stood all by itself like a monolith, right on the beach. It was, and still is, the most spectacular place we've stayed. There were only two apartments on the 25th floor, so ours wrapped around half the building with windows on three sides and terraces on two sides. The terrace off the living room, kitchen and master bedroom overlooked the beach and an active Surf Club. The ensuite bathroom was a little disconcerting at first glance. It had floor to ceiling windows with no blinds or curtains, just a view of the city below and the towers of Surfers Paradise in the distance. I was a little reluctant to drop my pants in there the first time, until I realized that no other building was as tall as this one and no one could possibly see in. It was quite liberating to step out of the shower and stand naked in the sunshine in front of the window, enjoying the view as I dried off. No need to take the Reader's Digest into this biffy, the world outside is interesting enough. The Queen on HER throne couldn't have a better view.

The terrace just outside the kitchen was to become our favorite place to sit. There was a table and chairs there where we could eat our meals and some comfortable upholstered deck chairs to watch the happenings on the beach below. The beach curved away in both directions and we could see the town of Coolangatta in one direction and Surfers Paradise in the other. Just below us on the beach was a Surf Club and there was always something going on there. Our first morning in the condo we woke up to a faint buzzing noise and went in search of it. It turned out to be a Zamboni-like machine smoothing and compacting the sand on the beach. There were already surfers riding the waves and kayakers out beyond in the smoother water. We went to make some coffee to enjoy while we watched the activity and couldn't find a coffeemaker. All we could find was four bottles of instant coffee in the cupboard, which is horrible stuff in our opinion, so it was time to go shopping. We found a K-Mart not far from the condo and bought a basic drip coffeemaker for around $20, and a pound of coffee to go with it. We were surprised to find a K-Mart there as they had closed all their stores back home a few years previously.

A funny story about the coffeemaker – we couldn't take it with us when we left, so just left it in the condo with a package of coffee and a note that said "Enjoy". About a month later, after Bill and Jackie got back from their trip and visited the condo again, we got an e-mail from Bill thanking us very much for the coffeemaker and saying it made such good coffee that he was going to take it back home with him to enjoy every day. It seemed funny to us, that a guy who owned a million-dollar condo, a mansion in Brisbane and half a dozen cars would get so excited over a $20 coffeemaker. But if all they drank was instant, it's quite possible that he never had a decent cup of coffee before.

For all its luxury, this was the first place we had problems with internet. Keep in mind that this was the winter of 2005/2006 and wireless modems were a rarity in private homes. So far, every place we stayed had wired internet. In those we simply unplugged the ethernet cable from the back of their computer and plugged it into our laptop. As this condo was a vacation place that they mainly used on weekends, they didn't even have a computer here. We were prepared for this, so we had an AOL e-mail account with dial-up access. Before leaving home, we were able to find the local AOL access numbers in Sydney, Adelaide and Brisbane, but none in the smaller areas such as Burleigh Heads. This meant that we had to use the access number in Brisbane, which was long distance at 25 cents a minute. This was a bit pricey when we were doing e-mail, writing a blog and uploading to our personal website, not to mention doing our banking and paying our bills from back home. So, on one of our first trips to a mall we set up a temporary account with a local phone company and bought prepaid internet at $1.00 an hour. Still dial-up, but affordable. It took a while to get it set up and working as the condo phone went through a switchboard so it took an extra step to get through. We had to add the 9 for an outside line, and insert 2 commas, to cause a small pause for the switchboard to actually connect to an outside line before dialing the access number. With today's high-speed wireless modems, that sounds like the horse-and-buggy days of internet, and it really wasn't that long ago.

The other thing we had to shop for was a new hat for Doug. Somewhere over the previous week he lost his treasured Tilley hat. He may have left it on the plane or on one of the airport shuttles. We checked with both, but no hat like his was turned in. So, someone, somewhere, has a nice, almost new Tilley hat. The hat shop where we went, to our surprise, actually sold Tilley hats, but they were more than double the Canadian price. He bought a "Tilley style" clone at a fraction of the price, and had to look for a new Tilley when we got home. The new hat didn't look quite the same but kept the Aussie sun off his neck and ears, so that was the important thing.

We had another interesting experience at the mall when we went to McDonald's for coffee. This one had something we'd never seen before, a McCafe attached. It had all the fancy coffees, lattes, mochas, frappes, etc., and delicious desserts like chocolate mud cake, cherry cheesecake, carrot cake and banana bread. It was another couple of years before we got a McCafe in our McDonald's back home, and they still don't have those desserts.

We'd been checking out the things to do in this area, but decided not to cram as much into every day as we did before. Our stay here was a month so we had lots of time to do things. Besides, just sitting on the terrace and watching the happenings on the beach below was a never-ending entertainment.

The nearest town to our condo was Surfer's Paradise. It was totally touristy, with souvenir shops alternating with pubs, and neon signs everywhere. Even the beach was lined with places selling food or renting equipment. We didn't stay long, but driving back along the shore road we came across a Surf Club and went in. It had a beautiful big clubhouse with a restaurant overlooking the beach, with lots of tables outside on a terrace. We checked their programs and they had entertainment several times a week and draws and raffles on Tuesdays and Fridays, as well as Happy Hour most days. And their wine prices by the bottle in the restaurant were cheaper than the liquor stores - quite a contrast from most restaurants. They also had bingo twice a week, and after grappling with it the first few times, I'd come to enjoy their weird bingo. It looked so good that we decided to buy a month's membership. The reason we decided on this one rather than the Surf Club on the beach right in front of us, was because it was entertainment oriented. The club near us, although it was within walking distance and we occasionally went to its restaurant, was very heavily into sports. There were swimming and kayaking classes all day, with competitions every weekend. It had very few of the social amenities that the club near Surfer's had.

One day we went for a walk on the beach in front of our building. We'd been watching the beach for a few days from 25 floors up, seeing the tides and the Surf Life Saving people practising, as well as the surfers and kayakers. We were finally getting to see the people up close and to look up at our building from below. We also waded in the ocean, but only up to our knees as we had no wish to be shark food. It was interesting to wade in the South Pacific; the last ocean we had waded in was the North Atlantic. Different hemisphere and definitely different temperature.

That beach in front of us was to fascinate us the whole month we were there. As soon as we got up in the morning, we sat out on the terrace with our coffee to watch what was happening on the beach. There were people there as early as 6 am, walking and running on the sand. The sand near the water was so hard-packed that the trucks carrying surfboards and equipment drove on it all the time. The sand above the high-watermark was softer so that's why they used the Zamboni-like machine to compact it and smooth it before the day's crowds arrived. One day we thought there was a shark scare as we heard the sharp sound of a whistle and everyone came charging out of the water. Then for the next half hour the Zodiacs patrolled just offshore. They must have given the all-clear as the swimmers went right back in as before.

One day we took the bus to Byron Bay, which was a very special experience.

The Byron Bay lighthouse is perched on the most easterly point of land in Australia, jutting out into the Pacific Ocean. Five months previously, on our driving trip across Canada, we visited Cape Spear lighthouse, near St. John's, Newfoundland, the most easterly point of North America. So within five months, we've stood at the base of two lighthouses, on the most easterly point of two different continents, looking across two different oceans, in two different hemispheres. In each case there were thousands of miles between where we were standing and the nearest land on the other side.

When I was a little girl growing up in Port aux Basques, Newfoundland, within spitting distance of the ocean, I never dreamed I would travel so far, see so many things and have so many different experiences. When I would sit on our front steps, watching the waves crash over the rocks at the base of Channel head lighthouse, and listen to the mournful sound of the foghorn, I never thought I would see the waves crash at the base of another lighthouse on the other side of the world. Travel is so much easier now than it was even that short time ago; I wonder what the next half century will bring? Unfortunately, I'll never know. But I hope my grandchildren have the joy of discovering far-flung places as I have. And Home Swapping has definitely helped us to afford it.

Over the next few weeks, we really enjoyed the Surf Club we joined. On Mondays and Wednesdays, they had a members' $10 special. For that we got a full dinner with four choices of meat, a glass of beer or wine with dinner, and a $2.00 credit for the pokies (poker machines). The very first day we took advantage of that special we put our $2 credits into adjacent machines and Doug won $9, while I won $15. So we got our dinner for free. Free is good!

Another day I went to play Bingo in the morning and won two games, for $50 and $20. When Doug came to pick me up, he suggested I use the $70 to buy a new suitcase as mine was in bad shape. After our last flight the handle didn't retract and one wheel was loose and wobbly. Then the shuttle driver in Sydney ripped off one of the handles. That sounded like a good idea, so off we went to the mall and bought a nice large lightweight bag, being careful to stay within the airlines size requirements. It was a blue denim with colored swirls on it. I hate black luggage; it all looks the same on the carousel, and it's a wonder that most people seem to get their correct one.

One day we drove into Surfer's Paradise to see a new attraction that was advertised. It was called Infinity and was billed as a sensory experience. It was that. It was also weird and a little claustrophobic. We walked through a maze of mirrors, flashing lights, see-through glass floors with moving objects right under our feet, complete darkness, moving and uneven floors, a moving hanging bridge, a room full of big plastic balls and other sensations that confused the eyes and perception. It was interesting, but I wasn't sure it was worth the cost.

One thing we didn't enjoy there was the TV. Any time we found a regular show that we usually watched back home, the episode was over a year old. We tended to mostly watch documentaries on the History or Discovery channels. One documentary we saw was very familiar to us. It was about icebergs off the coast of Newfoundland and the danger they present to the offshore oil rigs on the Hibernia oil field.

Something different that we did virtually every time we visited Australia was go to a Mole Scan Clinic to check for skin cancer. As Australia has the world's highest incidence of skin cancers, including melanoma, they have these scan clinics everywhere. They are store-front clinics in shopping centers where you can make an appointment and go anytime. For Aussies it is covered by Medicare, but we had to pay $50. We thought it was little enough to pay for peace of mind. The same thing in Canada would have to be done by a dermatologist and appointments made probably months ahead.

One day while we were at Burleigh Heads, Doug and Terry, our hosts in Brisbane, came to visit. It was nice to see them again. We later were to visit with them during two other exchanges, one in Melbourne when they brought baby Daniel with them, and again a couple of years later on our last exchange to Australia in Maroochydore.

Although the view from the 25th floor was great on a sunny day, during a storm it was fascinatingly scary. We had several thunderstorms during our stay there and the pyrotechnics were spectacular. Despite the storms there was still a lot of activity on the beach below us. The local people didn't seem to mind what the weather conditions were; if they came to the beach to swim, that's what they were going to do. The only thing that got them out of the water was a shark report, and then only reluctantly.

From our lofty viewpoint we often saw sharks, mostly far off-shore, but a few times alarmingly close. One morning we looked out to see the beach crowded with people and no one in the water. Then we saw why. The water was dark with schools of baitfish called Pilchards. When the baitfish come in close to shore the sharks always follow. The whole beach is usually on alert for a few days before the baitfish show up as the helicopter shark patrol keeps tabs on where they are, with predictions on their movements.

From our terrace we could see quite far out and see what the people on the beach couldn't. We could see dark forms in the water, and occasionally the water getting stirred up, so we could pinpoint where the sharks were. Right then we wished we had some sort of communication with the beach as we saw one man in the water surfing and he was dangerously close to the action. Finally, someone yelled at him and he came out of the water. Later in the day we saw gulls gathering in groups feeding on the surface and occasionally a great splashing and churning of the water, so we figured the sharks got some of the birds as well. It was an awesome display of nature's food chain and one of Australia's most unfriendly critters.

About halfway through our stay there we went on a bus tour up into the hinterland, the occupied land away from the coast. Our guide referred to the area as "the green behind the gold", meaning the green rainforest beyond the golden sand or Gold Coast. The tour went up into the hills, up 16% grades with steep drop-offs with no barriers! Scary, but the views were fabulous. There were also waterfalls, some of them quite high with short hikes to get to them. We also went to a tropical fruit farm where we tasted some quite different fruits, some we had never heard of before, let alone tasted. There was Jack Fruit that grows up to 30kg in weight with a tough spiny rind. There was Soursop and Red Dragon Fruit. I quite liked the Red Dragon and bought one. Then we had ice cream with our choice of fruit blended in. I chose red dragon, pineapple and passion fruit. It was the best ice cream I had ever tasted!

When we got back from our tour of the hinterland there was a message on our phone from Keith and Ann, who planned to arrive the next day, so we had company again for a while.

The next day, which was Valentine's Day, Keith and Ann arrived with their friends Ron and Mary from Brisbane. They were a very nice couple and we could see why K & A got along with them. We sat out on the terrace most of the afternoon, drinking wine and shark watching, then went to a Japanese restaurant for dinner.

The next day, two days after Valentine's Day, started with a bang. In my e-mail there was one from our son Pete. He and Natalie, and a couple of friends were holidaying in the Dominican Republic. He announced that he and Natalie were engaged! As near as we could tell from his message and the time difference, he proposed on Valentine's Day, on a beach, in the moonlight. We never realized he was such a romantic. Needless to say, we were delighted.

The condo had a barbecue grill outside, so one night we cooked a heavier meal than usual, pork chops, baked potatoes and corn. All this was after Happy Hour, so we were quite stuffed. After this heavy meal, Keith and Ann decided to go for a walk. They arrived back home an hour later laughing so hard they couldn't talk. When they finally told us the story, we were in stitches, laughing so hard my stomach hurt.

For background, in a hot humid climate like this, enclosed spaces get very stuffy and smelling of mildew, so a lot of elevators have air fresheners that emit a little puff at timed intervals. Apparently, as they got back from their walk, Keith's digestive system was working at full tilt, and in the elevator on the way up there was a large passing of gas. Just at that moment the air freshener gave a hiss and emitted its regular puff.

"Oh my," says Keith," this is a classy place that Doug and Helen are living in. The elevator automatically detects farts and deodorizes them." Ann broke up and they were still laughing when they arrived.

We predict that the story of the elevator with the automatic fart detector will go down in the annals of family history.

One day while Keith and Ann were with us, Keith did a Don Quixote imitation. Only it was with a ceiling fan instead of windmills. The condo had ceiling fans in every room and Keith took off his shirt, pulling it straight up over his head, forgetting that he was standing right below the fan. As his hand shot up it connected with the fan with a loud whack. Lucky for him it was one of the fans with plastic paddles instead of metal, so he still has his fingers, although they were cut and bruised.

Both Keith and Ann loved the area we were in but decided that they wanted their own space if they were going to stay for a while, so they went apartment hunting and found one in nearby Coolangatta they could rent for two weeks.

The last couple of days they were with us we did some serious sightseeing. One day we went to Currumbin Wildlife Park to see some native animals: kangaroos, koalas, wombats and Tasmanian devils. We also saw a demonstration of handling deadly snakes, but we weren't sure why anyone would even want to do that. Another day we went to Lamington National Park. We're not sure which came first, Lamington Park, or those little coconut covered cakes called Lamingtons that are the Australian national sweet. One very interesting feature of Lamington Park was a hike through the rain forest to a swinging bridge suspended high in the tree tops. It was literally a bird's eye view of the forest. After the hike we watched a parrot show and one of the birds landed on my head and got his feet tangled in my hair. It was kind of a weird feeling and I just hoped that he wouldn't feel the need to poop while he was there. We also went to Mt. Tambourine and visited the Mt. Tambourine winery. We knew they had a wine called Black Shiraz, and as our daughter Kristal had a black cat named Shiraz we thought we might take her back a bottle. However, it was quite expensive so Doug tasted it first and was glad he did. It was awful, very harsh and acidic. Living in Kelowna, the home of award-winning wines, has spoiled us. We won't put up with bad wines just because they have a high price tag.

Instead, we just talked one of the staff into giving us a label to take back. We told her we had no luggage room, omitting how bad the wine actually was.

One evening we got a phone call from our son Pete in Toronto. It was 10 pm at night in Australia, but 7 am the next morning in Toronto. In just over a week, he and Natalie had made quite a few plans for their wedding. The wedding date was to be August 14 and it would be a destination wedding at Lake Louise in Alberta, one of Pete's favorite places. The wedding would be preceded by three days of hiking, mountain biking and golf. We told him to expect us on day three! I should add here that both Pete and Natalie are athletes who had already run several marathons together, and most of their friends were the same. In fact, the guest list at the August wedding included two Olympic gold medalists. Over the next week or so we got several e-mails with wedding plans. The wedding party was planned for four days, with events scheduled every day. Some of the more adventurous will go on an 8-hour hike and a day of mountain biking, but sightseeing and walking a golf course will be more our speed.

When Keith and Ann moved into their apartment in Kirra Beach, near Coolangatta, we expected to miss them, but in reality, we saw them almost every day, as they were only a 20-minute drive or bus ride away.

One of the more interesting aspects of home swap is that we are not living as tourists. We're living in a regular house or apartment with neighbors. And we're grocery shopping and doing regular things as the locals would. We do things and meet people that we never would if we were staying in a hotel. As we have a car, we go places we normally wouldn't if we were relying on buses.

We were having lunch at the Surf Club one day and got into a conversation with a couple at the next table. They were from Perth, which is where we planned to go on our next trip to Australia. We asked a lot of questions about the area and ended up exchanging names and addresses, and also got their phone number in Perth, as they said to contact them if we did get there. They were fascinated by home exchanging and asked us questions about that, so we gave them the Australian web address. Their accents were slightly different, so we asked about it and found out that he was an Aussie, originally from Northern Australia, and she was a Maori from New Zealand. He had lived many years in New Zealand and had acquired an accent that was neither Aussie nor Kiwi but somewhere in between. They were a really interesting couple that we hoped we'd meet up with again sometime.

We found the weather in Australia to be really interesting, and not just for the reversal of the seasons. A blistering hot Christmas Day in Brisbane was an experience, but we expected that. However, living high above the ground on the 25th floor was quite different, especially when the weather was not sunny. One morning we woke up to nothing outside our windows, just a blank whiteness. Even the railing on the terrace, which was only about six feet away from us, was fading, and further down the terrace was completely invisible. Walking outside everything felt chilly and damp. Although we could see nothing, we could hear perfectly, perhaps even better than usual. We could hear the life saving crew on the beach calling to each other as they did their daily exercises. We could hear people talking and even gulls squawking. But it was as if we were wrapped in a huge batch of cotton batting. Living on the coast, as we both did as children, we'd often experienced fog, but never that thick and dense.

That part of Australia essentially has two seasons. Winter and summer are almost indistinguishable so the two seasons are The Wet and The Dry. That's what you hear them referred to as "last year during the wet it was cooler" or "two dry's ago we had so many wildfires". While we were in Burleigh Heads it was the start of the wet. The weather pattern was quite predictable; hot and sunny most of the day, then about 4 or 5 pm clouds would roll in and we might have a thunderstorm. Then it would rain off and on most of the night. We would wake up to a shower and then the clouds would disappear and it would be hot and sunny again for the rest of the day. One morning we watched a storm do something we had never seen before, and were lucky enough to get some photos of it. We were up at 7 am and saw a storm front advancing across the water towards us with a rainbow on its leading edge. Standing on the terrace just outside our bedroom we felt the first few drops of rain. Our terrace curved around the building from the living room on the east side to the bedroom on the north. We watched the storm lashing against our bedroom windows for a while, then went and made breakfast. Half an hour later the sun was shining and when we went out on the terrace off the living room it was perfectly dry. I walked along the terrace and the wet part started about halfway around, so we were right on the edge of the storm. The road below us was dry and the wet road started about two blocks away. So, the rain that hit us at the top of the building didn't strike the ground for another two blocks. Another interesting phenomenon – the rainbow we saw was below us.

Shortly after that storm we saw our highest ever tide. The beach in front of us was usually between 100 to 200 feet wide, depending on the tide. Then one morning when we looked out the water was only about 10 feet from the grassy bank. No one was walking on the sand, everyone was walking on the wooden walkways just above the beach. Strangely enough, the next tide was normal again.

2006 was an Olympic year and we watched the Olympics on TV a few times with Keith and Ann. However, it was not as interesting to us as watching at home as we saw very few Canadians compete. We were happy to hear that a Newfoundland curling team, representing Canada, won a gold medal, but we didn't get to see any of the games. I guess Australian TV execs thought there would be no interest in a game played with brooms on ice.

One day during our last week there Keith and Ann called and invited us to dinner as their friends, Ron and Mary from Brisbane, were coming for a visit. We had a great dinner and a few bottles of wine were emptied that evening. So many, in fact, that we left our truck there and took the bus home.

Our exchange agreement for Burleigh Heads was for the month of February, and as we got down to the last few days, we realized we would be sorry to leave that condo. It was easily the nicest place we had stayed and definitely the most interesting.

Our next exchange was two weeks at Lyle and Val's condo at Magic Mountain. It was also on the Gold Coast and only about 10 minutes drive from the one we were leaving. We had to make a couple of trips to get all our stuff there as besides our very full suitcases we had several bags of groceries and items like shampoo, paper towels and toilet paper that we would need there, but definitely wouldn't be going home with us.

We also had our usual two boxes of wine. We'd been drinking mostly wine there as the Australian wine is so good and they put some of their best wine in 4 liter boxes. I found a Traminer Reisling that was one of the best wines I had ever tasted. It was sold in a 4 liter box with a spout, and cost $13.99. I made sure to have some in the fridge the whole time we were there. Doug bought a box of Cabernet Merlot for a dollar more, and it also was on the shopping list whenever it ran low. We were wishing we could bring back a couple of boxes but our limit, unfortunately is only one liter each. Somehow it seems unfair that the customs limit is the same for us, who were away three months, as it is for someone away only a week. But no one ever said that government regulations always made sense.

After we made the last trip and got our things organized in the new condo, Doug drove the truck back to Burleigh Heads and parked it in the underground garage, left the keys with the front desk as arranged and took the bus to our new place. I think he was sorry to give up the truck as he loved driving it.

One thing you always do when leaving an exchange home is to clean it and leave it in the condition you got it. The day we left we spent the morning cleaning the inside, but realized that all the windows that were sparkling clean when we arrived were now grungy and streaked with salt spray. There was no way we could clean all those windows as they were floor to ceiling and we couldn't reach the tops of most. So we arranged with the front desk to have a cleaning service do the windows after we left. It was very little to pay to live in such a lovely place for a month.

Our new apartment at Magic Mountain was very nice with a balcony overlooking the pool. Our only glitch was that the car that went with the new place wouldn't start. Doug thought the battery was dead, but after a quick call to Lyle we found out the battery had been disconnected to prevent it going dead while sitting in the garage for several months. Doug hooked it up and got it going and then familiarized himself with the gears. He'd been spoiled so far with cars that were automatic, but this one was standard transmission so had gears to contend with. By this time, he was used to driving on the left, but changing gears with the left hand was still a challenge.

Shortly after we moved to the Magic Mountain condo we had dinner with Keith and Ann for a last time as they were leaving soon for New Zealand. We went to Coolangatta to one of the largest RSL clubs we've ever seen. We went on a Thursday night which is free wine night. As we always say – free is good. It was also the first time we had ever seen cooked-to-order steaks on a buffet. We were sorry to see Keith and Ann go as we'd enjoyed the time we spent with them in Australia. Keith is my younger brother, eight years younger than me. With this age difference we were not friends as children, and he was just a kid of 10 when I left home. Over the years we saw each other occasionally when I went home for a visit, but it wasn't until much later in life that we connected and became friends as well as siblings. Since he retired, we've become closer as Keith and Ann love to travel as much as Doug and I do, and we have occasionally travelled together, or met up someplace as we did in Australia. Two years after our Australian trip we went on a cruise of the Mediterranean with them.

We mentioned before that you sometimes have a problem when living in someone else's home and this time it was a fridge thinking it was a freezer. Our second day there we were watching the evening news on TV when we heard a bang from the kitchen. We searched all over but didn't find anything. Then about 10 minutes later there was another, much louder, bang and Doug said he thought it came from the fridge. When we opened the fridge there was brown liquid everywhere, covering everything inside. On the bottom shelf was a can of cola, split open down the side and about half full of brown slush. It had apparently frozen and the first bang was the snap-top popping and the second was the can splitting down the side. Everything in the fridge had to be washed off, as did all the racks and the entire inside. In the process an egg got broken and added to the mess. Half an hour later, we'd missed most of the TV news but the fridge got an unscheduled cleaning. We noticed that the temperature dial was set at about half, so we turned it down to one-quarter, and that seemed to solve the problem.

Our first week at Magic Mountain we didn't do much and certainly didn't do any sightseeing or beach walking. It was the worst and wildest weather of the entire trip and was later named on the local news as the "no-name cyclone". It had all the properties of a cyclone but was never officially named by the weather office. The winds were clocked at 100km per hour with waves between 20 and 30 feet high. There had been a surfing competition scheduled at Surfer's Paradise, but it was cancelled as the waves were deemed too dangerous. However, some of the surfers couldn't resist the challenge. They showed a news clip on TV of some surfers taking jet skis out into the surf to have some fun and having to be rescued. They showed an upside-down jet ski being tossed in the waves. The beach Life Savers, who had to risk their own lives to rescue them, were later on TV calling the surfer's actions "incredibly stupid". The storm had other repercussions as well. There were washouts along the beaches and slippage on cliffs, floods in beachfront homes and lots of accidents on the roads. It was a good time to stay home and do things like laundry. The biggest and most long-lasting damage was to the beaches. A lot of them lost quite a bit of their sand. Beaches that previously had sloped gently from parks and walkways, now had six-foot drop-offs from grass to sand where the waves had gouged out chunks of beach. In some places there were rocks showing that only the previous week had been buried under several feet of sand. They said the sand would come back over the next few months but it looked rather bare at that point.

Around this time we had to start wrapping up our Australian adventure and thinking about the next part of our trip. We'd planned to stay in Hong Kong for three days. This was a city we'd always heard about and wanted to visit, so flying through it to visit Australia seemed like a golden opportunity for a stopover. We thought we'd have no trouble finding Hong Kong dollars but the first two banks we went to had none. We asked if they'd order some, but apparently that was a service reserved for regular customers and not drop-ins. We thought that was not very good PR. Someone else in the line-up suggested we try the Thomas Cook agency in the mall, so that's what we did and were successful there. Although our hotel and airport transfers were paid for in advance, and we could use credit cards for meals and shopping, we felt we needed some local cash for tips and sightseeing, and of course, shopping in the street markets.

Early in our visit to Australia we had heard about the deep-sea fishing and how much could be caught in one trip. Somehow it slipped through the cracks of planning until our last week. Doug finally booked his fishing trip when we had only about four days left. I had instructed him to bring home his catch all cleaned and filleted. I like cooking and eating fish, but I'm not interested in the messy bits. However, there was no catch. They fished all morning and caught nothing. Apparently, storms affect the fish and it takes a while after a storm for the fish to come back. Of course, the charter boat owner didn't tell them that until they'd paid their money and were well out to sea. Incidentally, the fishing boat left from a pier north of Labrador. And no, we weren't transported to a place in northern Canada. The suburb just north of Surfer's Paradise is called Labrador. And while we're on the subject of names, the Gold Coast has towns called Miami Beach and Palm Beach, and a housing development called Cypress Gardens. Someone responsible for naming places must have visited Florida. Also, a lady I met playing bingo told me she lived in Toronto, which is a suburb of Sydney.

That night we decided to go online and check out our flight to Hong Kong, to see if there had been any changes in time. We discovered that we had the absolute worst seats on the plane, the very back row that didn't recline and right next to the toilets. I couldn't change the seats online, so called the next day and got them changed to a window and aisle in a row with only two seats. Much better!

The second last night before we left, H and M, friends of our hosts who live in this same complex invited us for dinner. They are also home exchangers who have been to Canada, so we had an interesting dinner and conversation. I also asked if they knew of a place like our Goodwill where we could donate some clothes. We both came with full suitcases and have done some shopping along the way, so something has to go. M said she has a place that she donates used items and was planning to take them a box next week, so to leave it with her and she would look after it. We left her a huge bag of clothes from both of us, so hope she wasn't too shocked at how much she had to dispose of.

Chapter 6

A HONG KONG EXPERIENCE

WE LEFT AUSTRALIA ON March 15 after our longest exchange so far. We had a short one-hour flight to Cairns and then seven hours to Hong Kong. Since this was a day flight there was no sleeping and even though Cathay Pacific is great about entertainment and food, any flight starts to drag after about five hours. The only funny thing that happened during the flight was when someone mentioned "the Ides of March" and we both realized that it was Doug's birthday. Both of us had totally forgotten.

We had a shuttle booked to pick us up at the airport and take us to the hotel, the Novotel Century Harbour View. There we received the best news of the day; we'd been upgraded to a harbour view suite. It was a lovely suite, two rooms, two bathrooms and two beds, one of which was an extra long. That made Doug happy. There were also huge windows with a great view of the city lights and the harbour.

Hong Kong was an experience that we absolutely have to write about, even though technically it wasn't part of our exchange. We started our day with a huge breakfast in the hotel dining room which was included in our room rate. Then we went on a Hong Kong city tour that was also part of our package. We really enjoyed the tour, seeing a lot of the city, taking a sampan ride on the harbour, visiting the market and the highest peak in the city to enjoy the view. We saw the high buildings in the city from the peak, but just the tops jutting out of the smog. We couldn't see the harbour at all.

The sampan ride was an experience not to be missed. There were sampans everywhere, as private boats, tour boars, work boats carrying freight and as living quarters for some people. The harbour also had mooring space for several hundred huge private yachts. And our sampan driver was an experience in itself, or herself. She couldn't have been much over 4 ½ feet tall, but she ruled the harbour. Someone on the tour referred to her as the Dragon Lady. She drove that sampan like a sports car and everyone else got out of her way. She yelled at people as she passed them and they yelled back. Twice she left the helm and let the boat drive itself and did something like wash the front of the boat or just stood at the back and yelled at someone. That she didn't ram other boats was more to their credit than hers. She stopped the boat before it got back to the dock and demanded her fee from everyone, then counted it several times before she was satisfied. And we all knew for a certainty that if she was short even $1 we weren't going to dock until she got it. Then she shoved a tip bucket in front of the stairs where we practically had to trip over it to get off the boat. She was worth her fee and the tips just for the entertainment value.

The market was an experience also, but this time for sticker shock. The value of the HK$ at that time was roughly 6 to 1, $6HK equaled $1US. When I first saw a cup of coffee for $10 and an ice cream cone for $24, it was a shock until I did the math and realized the coffee was only $1.75 and the ice cream $4 in our currency. Then some things, especially manufactured goods and fabrics were so cheap that I had to do the math twice to be sure. For instance, I bought a black shawl for $50HK. It was 80% wool and 20% silk and was so soft and silky and warm that I would happily have paid that much in US$, but it actually cost me only $8.50. Then I hit my best bargain of the day. I saw something I really wanted and had intended purchasing if I could find one at a good price. It was a rack of pure silk scarves. From several yards away, I thought it said $100, which would come out to about $18US. If I could find a scarf I liked that was a price I was willing to pay. Then with a closer look I saw the sign read 6 for $100. That would bring the price down to around

$3 for an item that would cost me upwards of $40 at home, so I immediately began thinking Christmas and Birthday gifts. As that store also had t-shirts for $36 (read $6 each) I also bought one of those. I was such a good customer that the woman selling them took $5 off the shirt and threw in an extra scarf, making it 7 for $100. So, I bought a t-shirt and silk scarf for myself and six gifts to take home for a total of about $25. Shopping doesn't get much better than that.

I still, however, continued to get sticker shock and spent most of my time in Hong Kong doing math in my head every time I saw a price tag. Our second night in Hong Kong there was a buffet dinner at our hotel. It was $179HK, but as it was ladies' night mine was 50% off. We figured it came to around $60 in our currency for both of us, and we've spent more than that for dinner in a good restaurant at home. The dinner was different in another way. We have never eaten so much unidentified food before. It was a buffet and nothing was labelled, so I just put food on my plate having no idea what it was. Most of it was delicious, and if the occasional item wasn't, well… call it an experience. The good far outweighed the yuk. The dessert table was decadent and varied. I thought they couldn't fool me on desserts but there were at least two items on my plate I couldn't identify. You know I got my money's worth at that buffet, no matter what the currency was. Incidentally, 10 years later the exchange rate hadn't changed much. In 2006 it was 6 to 1, in 2017 it was 7 ½ to 1.

Our city tour on our first day showed us the modern city of Hong Kong, but our second day was quite different. We got to see some ancient Chinese culture and also learned just how different and special Hong Kong is.

On the first part of our tour we visited the New Territories, on the mainland north of Hong Kong. The New Territories are actually the oldest occupied part of Hong Kong, dating back almost 6,000 years. Why the Old is called New was never satisfactorily explained. We visited a Buddhist monastery that houses the three largest Buddha statues in Hong Kong. These were holy Buddhas in an active monastery. Later we visited a couple of others that were no longer holy places, but belonged to one of the five founding families of China.

Lastly, we visited the ancestral home of the Tang family, one of the founding five, and toured their ornate meeting hall and village. Our guide was a Tang and he showed us his personal ancestral shrine. It was a niche in the wall, with ornate gold and red carvings, hung with several hundred small wooden slats about two inches wide and eight inches long, hung in rows with writing on them. He pointed out the one that represented his grandfather and said that someday both his father and he would be hanging there with his ancestors. Then he added that he hoped that honor was a long way in the future. Then he took us to a village and showed us his house, a small narrow wooden structure, two floors high, attached to several other similar houses. We had a look inside his house and met his two dogs. He was a great guide and gave us a fascinating tour.

The things we learned that day: the name Hong Kong means Fragrant Harbour. We could think of a few more appropriate synonyms for fragrant; such as odor, smell, stink, stench or reek, but the Chinese tend to call things by positive names. The name Kowloon, which is the mainland part of the city, means Nine Dragons. Kow is nine and loon means dragon. The handover of Hong Kong from the British to China in 1997 had not affected the city financially. It was still a separate entity, financially and governmentally, with its own currency and law court. The disaster that was predicted never happened. They used the phrase "one country, two systems" and said that it had been guaranteed for 50 years until 2047.

After our tour we went for a walk along the streets near our hotel and found a shopping center. It was quite different from our shopping centers which are mostly on one level. This one was vertical, very small on the outside and only about a dozen stores on each level, but the building went up eight levels. The top level had only one store, a supermarket called Welcome. We walked through the supermarket, looking at all the different products and made a couple of purchases. The products in the store were an interesting combination of totally Chinese products, that we had no idea what they were unless there was a picture on the label, and products like Kraft salad dressings and Lipton soups in packages exactly like home but with the addition of Chinese characters on the label.

And then, on our last night in Hong Kong, my resident klutz, Doug, had an accident. We managed to go three months with nothing more than grazed knuckles and he had to go spill some blood in Hong Kong - and in a very embarrassing way.

After our elaborate Chinese dinner the previous night that gave us both indigestion, we opted for a simple dinner of take-out chicken. We had earlier spotted a KFC about a block from our hotel, so Doug went out to get some for us to eat in our room. He came back about half an hour later, dinner in hand, but bleeding from a cut over his eyebrow. He was quite shaky and said he needed my medical help before we ate. The stores, apparently, are not used to tall people. The restaurant had a glass door, framed in glass, and when he stepped up into the store from the sidewalk his head hit the glass door edge, resulting in a cut above and through his eyebrow about an inch long and quite deep. He said he was standing there, almost in shock from the blow and bleeding copiously and the staff rushed to help him. They washed his cut and bandaged it, and he came back, still a little shaky and asked me to look at it. The cut was quite deep and if we were home would probably need a couple of stitches, but it wasn't gaping open and could probably be held together with a band aid. My main concern was cleanliness; how clean was the glass door frame, and how well did they wash the cut.

We asked the front desk for directions to a pharmacy and went there to get some first aid stuff. At the pharmacy they didn't speak any English and we didn't know any Chinese, but with a bit of charades and picture drawing on paper, as well as an inspection of the cut by the pharmacists, we got what we needed and I was able to disinfect the wound and bandage it. In retrospect, the scene in the pharmacy was actually quite funny. There were three pharmacists, all female, all more than a foot shorter than Doug's 6'3", and they all had to inspect the cut. The only way that could be accomplished was for Doug to bend over at the waist with his hands on his knees, and his rear end stuck out, which at one point knocked something off a shelf. While they were inspecting the cut and discussing what was needed, I was looking around the store and spotted a product that used to be in my first aid kit but was now unavailable. It was mercurochrome, so I picked it up to include with our purchase. But when we tried to buy it, they refused to sell it to us. When I tried again to put it with our purchases one of them used a charade to tell me why. She touched the bottle, then her own eye, and then slammed her palm against her eye, effectively telling me the mercurochrome would damage his eye if it got into it. We got the message, so left without it.

The chicken, when we got around to it, was cold and greasy, but still good. KFC will never be the same. It still brings back memories of Hong Kong.

One other thing we did in Hong Kong was "beat the system", which is something I love to do on occasion. We wanted to check e-mail while we were there so inquired at the desk about internet. The cost for guests was $25 for 24 hours of internet. I asked if I could buy one hour for one dollar, but was told that $25 was the business package for internet, as this was essentially a business hotel. I decided not to take it. Then back in the room, I remembered that in my travel file I had an AOL local number for Hong Kong, as I'd gotten it at the same time as the Brisbane and Sydney local numbers. I then went online checked e-mail and answered a couple of them, as well as updated our blog, for 75 cents, the hotel's cost of a local phone call.

The next day we flew from Hong Kong to Vancouver, ending our longest exchange to date. We didn't travel very far between exchanges as all three were in the state of Queensland, quite close together, but we also got to spend some time in Sydney and Adelaide. And then there was our stopover in Hong Kong to add to the experience.

After a couple of years of intense travelling, we decided for the winter of 2007 to take a rest from long flights and drove to Arizona for a month instead. We also didn't want to be out of touch with our son and daughter-in-law as they were expecting our first grandchild in early March. Instead, we enjoyed our first family Christmas in many years. Our daughter, Kristal, and son-in-law Brian came from Vancouver, and son Pete with a very pregnant Natalie came from Toronto. In January we left for Arizona, rented a condo and stayed there until mid-February.

Our first grandchild, Kacey Sierra, was born on March 13, just two days before her grandfather's birthday. A month later they announced they had just purchased their first house and we offered to fly to Toronto and help with the packing and moving. Natalie, still recovering from the birth and tired from sleepless nights and breastfeeding, happily accepted our offer. We spent three weeks there in April and May, packing up everything in their rented duplex and then unpacking in the new house. We went back again in September for a couple of weeks to look after Kacey while Pete and Nat took a much-needed holiday. As Kacey now recognized us and knew who we were, on our return home we set up a Skype account and talked to them every week. That was our way of ensuring she wouldn't forget who we were if we went a long time between visits. We subsequently used Skype to keep in touch for our next couple of years of travelling.

Chapter 7

THREE COUNTRIES, TWO CONTINENTS, ONE BIG ADVENTURE

DURING THIS YEAR OF no foreign travel, we were also planning the next winter with what turned out to be our longest and most complicated exchange.

We already had the month of February, 2008, planned for an exchange to Melbourne, Australia. The previous winter, we received an e-mail asking us if we would like an exchange to Melbourne the next February. The couple, Rob and Sue, said they were currently in Kelowna and loved the skiing so much they wanted to return the next year, but their current hosts were not interested in returning to Australia again so soon. When we received the email we were still in Arizona, so asked for the phone number where they were staying and we would call them when we returned. We said we were interested, and when we returned home we invited them to dinner and spent a delightful evening exchanging stories about our adventures in home swapping all over the world. We ended the evening by agreeing on the next February for our exchange and did all the paperwork right then. It was the only time we ever agreed to an exchange in person.

One place we really wanted to visit was Perth on the west coast of Australia, so started looking for an exchange a year ahead. We couldn't find anything at first, so when we got an offer from a couple in New Zealand, we decided to change from Perth to New Zealand instead. During the negotiations, we found out that the NZ couple were not skiers and would prefer to come to our place in the summer. They had a vacation home on Lake Taupo, one of the North Island's most popular spots which they offered to us for three weeks. We had done a non-simultaneous exchange once before with Val and Lyle from Ballarat, so checked our schedule to see what we could work out. We realized that Doug had a special class reunion that he wanted to attend in Bridgewater, Nova Scotia, the next summer. So, by spending a couple of weeks in Nova Scotia then a week with Pete, Nat and Kacey in Toronto, we could offer our empty house In Kelowna to the New Zealand couple for three weeks spanning August and September.

We agreed on the first three weeks in March as our time at Lake Taupo. They were not using it at that time and, as we'd been in New Zealand before in March, we liked the weather that time of year.

With February and March lined up, we now wanted an exchange for our coldest month, January, so we returned to our quest for an exchange in Perth and were successful this time. S and B had what they described as an 'outback' style house in a suburb of Perth on the edge of the national park. This house style, also called a 'Queensland' style, is popular in the outback and on ranches, but seldom found in a city. It is a square building, all on one level, with a roof peaked in the center and the slanting eaves extending up to six feet beyond the walls all the way around. This creates a veranda all around the house, usually with a raised wooden deck and railings. This six-foot roof over the veranda shades every room in the house from the sun and you can always find either a sunny side or a shady side to sit and rest. It's a perfect building style for a hot country. We were looking forward to experiencing it. We agreed to four weeks, January 3 to 31. Now all we had to do was arrange our flights.

With all our travelling in the previous few years, we thought we had enough points to travel to Australia on Air Canada in first class, which we were really looking forward to. However, we were a couple of thousand points short. Then, while we were on their website, we happened to notice that their partner, Singapore Airlines, required 5,000 points less for a first-class flight to Australia, and we had enough points for that . Upon checking their flight schedule, we found that we had to fly through Singapore if we used their airline, which would work out as Singapore is roughly directly north of Perth.

However, before we got into booking flights we ran into a major snag. S and B from Perth e-mailed us to say that, on checking flights, they found the cost far higher than they expected and their budget would not extend to that. But rather than cancel on us completely they would take an inexpensive two-week holiday to Bali from January 6 to 20, and if we still wanted to come, we could have their house for those two weeks. It wasn't exactly what we wanted, but better than nothing and our only chance of seeing Perth, so we agreed.

Up until now, we had always done our own booking of flights and hotels, but we realized that we now needed help coordinating our schedule and filling in the gaps. It was time to go see our travel agent.

We had previously used a very experienced agent named Annamarie when we booked a couple of groups from our seniors' community on cruises, so we went to see her and laid out our scheduling problem. We knew we had to do our own booking with the airline if we were travelling on points, but she helped us coordinate the dates and found us interesting things to fill in the gaps we now had between exchanges.

This is what she came up with.

As we had never been to Singapore before we would have liked to stay over a couple of days, but the type of flight we had didn't allow for stopovers. Annamarie found a way to get us a whole day and night in Singapore. Our flight arrived in Singapore at 11:00 pm with the flight onward to Perth leaving at midnight. As we were seniors, this was deemed as not enough time to make the departing flight, so we could stay overnight and take a flight the next day. There were several departing flights during the day, but the last one was at 8:30 pm and that's the one she recommended we book. As our time in Singapore was less than 24 hours it was considered as in-transit rather than a stopover. That gave us the night and all next day in the city. As we were in-transit we would not get our luggage, so she reminded us to have anything we might need for the night and all the next day in our carry-on bags. She booked us into the Holiday Inn near the airport and arranged for a shuttle pickup at the airport. She then arranged for a car and driver to pick us up at the hotel at 10:00 am the next morning, give us an all-day tour of the city and drop us back at the airport in time for our evening flight. This was something we had no way of knowing was possible and wouldn't have done on our own. We had talked about taking a couple of city tours, one in the morning and one in the afternoon. But as Annamarie explained, that was four separate tours and the cost of those would be almost as much as hiring the car and driver, and the car would give us more flexibility if we wanted to stay longer in one place. Plus, after the tours we would still have to find our own way to the airport. She was right. That day in Singapore is one of our favourite memories.

On our flight to Perth, although we had booked through Singapore Airlines, the first half of the trip was actually on Air Canada on a code share agreement. We flew Air Canada from Kelowna to Vancouver, a short 50-minute flight, and then Vancouver to Hong Kong. We had a wait of about 2 ½ hours in Vancouver between flights, but because we were flying first class we got to spend it in Air Canada's Maple Leaf Lounge, where we were able to get some breakfast. It had been a long time since we'd flown in first class, so we appreciated the comfortable seats with all the leg room. We actually had three windows in our space. They kept feeding us and offering us drinks for the next 14 hours to Hong Kong. However comfortable the seat and however good the service is, 14 hours in a plane is still a long time. We managed to sleep a little but probably only a couple of hours. Then after an hour on the ground in Hong Kong we got back on a plane for a five-hour flight to Singapore. This part of the flight was on Singapore Airlines, which we had heard was one of the best. I think what impressed us most was that, with only a glance at our seat numbers as we boarded, the flight attendant called us by name. We arrived in Singapore just after midnight and were met by a representative of Tour East, who took us to our hotel, the Holiday Inn Atrium. With a name like that I expected the hotel to be about five floors with an atrium in the middle. The reality was a 26 floor hotel and the center atrium went all the way from the lobby to a glass roof. What a view, inside and out. All the rooms opened onto walkways overlooking the atrium.

The next morning, we took full advantage of the hotel's buffet breakfast. Our printed itinerary for the day looked too crowded for lunch. We were picked up at 10 am by the car and driver we had hired and were surprised that it also included a guide. Terry, our guide, was good at his job. He got us to the most popular places either ahead of, or after, the big tour buses. There were two cruise ships in port that day so that was important.

The first place we went was the Orchid Park in the Botanical Gardens. We had no idea there was such a large variety of colors and varieties of orchids. One thing that fascinated me was that the exhibit included a Pitcher Plant. The Pitcher Plant is the provincial flower of Newfoundland, so it was a plant I was familiar with, but not this monster. In Newfoundland the Pitcher Plant is about a foot high, with a cone filled with toxic water that attracts and traps insects, which feed the plant. The Singapore version was eight feet high with a cone large enough to trap a small animal. I wouldn't like to encounter that one in the dark myself.

At our second stop, a local temple, I didn't know if I was being unnecessarily distrustful, but couldn't take the chance. Our guide explained that we were welcome to tour the temple, even though services were being conducted, but it was the custom to take off shoes, leave them outside, and enter the temple barefoot. I looked at the piles of black sandals and flipflops scattered around, and the people who were coming out and kicking other people's shoes around while looking for their own, or possibly a better pair. Then I looked at my own New Balance walking shoes with their custom orthotics, and decided there was no way I was taking them off and leaving them outside. Right then they were the only shoes I had; the others were in my luggage headed for Perth. I couldn't see myself walking barefoot the rest of the day, visiting Raffles Hotel and then walking on the plane and sitting in first class with my dirty bare feet. So, we just stood at the door and watched the proceedings, careful not to step over the threshold.

The best part of our day was probably the visit to the famous Raffles Hotel. I had read many stories over the years featuring Raffles and it was at the top of my list of places to visit in Singapore. It is a beautiful old white colonial building, built in a square with a courtyard in the center. Stores and restaurants lined the ground floor, but we were interested in only a couple of them. First was the Long Bar where we wanted to have a Singapore Sling, as this was where the drink originated. We invited our guide to have one with us and Doug almost fell off his chair when he got the bill - $74 for three Slings. However, the experience was worth it. The Long Bar is an original with dark wood and bevelled mirrors, a narrow circular staircase to the upper floor and large bamboo fans stirring the air. Then in the lobby was the famous Writers' Bar, where I just had to have my photo taken next to the brass sign. We had tea and scones in the café and then bought a couple of souvenirs in the Raffles shop. I could have ended my tour right there and been happy. However, our guide had a couple more things planned, including a Bum Boat ride on the Singapore River and a walk through a trendy market. Then we were taken to the airport to board Singapore Airlines again for a five-hour flight to Perth.

We arrived in Perth after midnight and took a taxi to our exchange house. That was actually the worst part of our whole trip. We didn't know where we were going and neither did the driver. I had a map and directions, but the driver took a wrong turn and got us completely lost. We drove around for almost an hour, and finally, between my map and his map and all of us watching street names and numbers, we finally got there.

The next morning we got a good look at the house where we would be staying for the next two weeks. True to its description, the veranda went around all four sides of the house, with a larger patio extension on one side with an outdoor table and chairs and a barbeque. The veranda was full of plants on all four sides and the south and west sides had drop-down shades to help cool the house. Just past the patio was a short pathway leading to a covered gazebo with wicker furniture, like an outdoor living room. That turned out to be our favourite place to sit in the shade and read. Behind the house was just bush, as it was situated on the edge of a national park.

Every exchange home has a welcome information book with important information about the house and the neighbours, with phone numbers to call "in case of". We had used those numbers a couple of times, like the house in Mooloolaba with the smoking dimmer switch. This house had information we had never encountered before or since. It was what to do in case of a bush fire nearby. Obviously fleeing was not an option, even though it would be our first instinct. There was a sprinkler system on the roof that was connected to a huge tank of water in the backyard, just beyond the gazebo. This tank was filled by roof runoff when it rained, and a small generator pumped it through the sprinkler system, soaking the roof in case of fire nearby with flying embers. There was also a machine called a reticulator, which had very detailed instructions in the info book. We'd never heard of it before, but it turned out to be the equivalent of our sprinkler system, except it used water from the holding tank and was only to be used if there was no rain for several days.

We also had a couple of pets, although only one, an elderly white cat, needed looking after. There was a cockatoo, a pink and gray Gallah, in a cage outside. He was not friendly to people he didn't know, so was looked after during our visit by a neighbour. There was also an aquarium with fish in the dining room, but all feed, lights and water maintenance were done automatically. Our only instruction on the fish was, "If a fish dies, scoop it out with a net and throw it out in the garden." Presumably the cat, or one of the birds or snakes from the nearby park would take care of disposal.

Our car at this house was an air-conditioned Hyundai. We were happy to see it was also automatic. Driving on the left is challenging enough without having to contend with a stick shift. We had to go out shopping right away as we needed groceries, as well as our usual supply of good Aussie wine.

The second day, a friend of our hosts, named Chris, came over as we were having a little trouble with the cat. He was afraid of us and wouldn't come in the house. She fed the cat, we opened the wine and had a good chat. We found out that the cat had his own cat door, so he came in the house during the night and ate his food.

Over the next few days we saw a lot of people walking in the bush behind the house, and realized that, as it was a park, there were probably some hiking trails that we might like to try. We asked Chris about access to the trails and she told us to only go on the weekend when there were a lot of other people walking as the pathways had lots of snakes when traffic was slow. As snakes are not Doug's favourite things, we decided to forego bush walking.

Most mornings we were awakened by the Aussie equivalent of a rooster, the Kookaburra. He's not a very big bird but he's loud. Sometimes he sounds like a baby crying and sometimes like someone laughing. Whichever noise he made, when it's right outside your window, you're done sleeping.

A couple of days later we discovered another annoyance, what we thought were mosquito bites were actually flea bites. Both of us had a dozen of the red, itchy bumps. We now wish the cat had stayed outside a little longer. We found a can of insect spray and thoroughly sprayed the carpets and furniture, as well as the floors. Then we went out to buy some itch cream. We blocked the cat door to keep him outside and shut our bedroom door in case he did get in. For the rest of the time we were there we shut him outside and fed him on the porch, making sure not to pet him or touch him in any way. As he was basically an outdoor cat, I don't think he minded.

We found ourselves enjoying using something we hadn't used before, a Tom-Tom GPS system in the car. Our host had programmed in the local supermarket, the shopping center, and of course, home. Any time we found ourselves getting lost we simply pressed "home" and it took us right back to the house. We had actually received one of these as a Christmas present from our son, Pete, but hadn't installed it before we left home. It was one of the first things we did when we got back home.

Since we knew we'd have no trouble getting back home, we felt comfortable exploring the city. Perth had a downtown pedestrian mall, called the Murray Street Mall. Two streets, Murray Street and Hay Street were both closed to traffic for about five blocks, which made shopping much more enjoyable. It's something that most Australian cities seem to have, and these outdoor shopping venues became our favorite places to walk and shop in whichever city we were in. We did not do much shopping in Perth however, except for necessities like groceries. Perth is the most expensive Australian city, probably because it is all by itself on the west coast and transportation costs are higher.

One day we went on a scouting trip for our last few days in Perth. We wanted to tour the Margaret River wine area, but it was about a three-hour drive outside the city, more than we wanted to drive, especially when tasting wine, so went looking for a tour. We decided on a two day tour our last two days in Perth, followed by a stay at a hotel near the railway station the night before boarding the Ocean Pacific train for our trip across the country.

About halfway through our stay in Perth we got an offer of an exchange in Germany for the next summer. This was very exciting for us as we had been trying for a Germany exchange for a while. Doug has a German name, and although his family has been in Canada for over two hundred years, the German heritage and customs on the south shore of Nova Scotia is still very strong. He grew up eating sausage and sauerkraut and most of his childhood friends also had German surnames. We had been in Germany a couple of times before, once on a bus tour and again as a stop on a cruise, but never long enough to get to know the country. He wanted to spend enough time in the country to research his German heritage.

We answered back that we were definitely interested and that June or July would be our preference. They replied that early summer wouldn't work for them and they wished to come in August. However, August wouldn't work for us as we were celebrating our

50th anniversary in August, we already had a big party planned and had family coming from all across the country, as well as some cousins from England. We proposed late August or early September. By the time we left Perth we still didn't have a definite date for that exchange, and weren't even sure it would happen. That's the way it is with home exchanges. It's something like a real estate deal, offers and counter-offers until an agreement is reached. Shortly after we arrived back home, we agreed on three weeks, the last week in August and the first two weeks in September. As we like to maximize our airfare by doing two things with one flight, we decided on a Danube River Cruise following the exchange. This cruise would be our 50th anniversary gift to ourselves. More about this exchange later.

Early in the planning for this trip to Perth, our very good friends and neighbours, Joan and Mike, gave us the name and phone number of Mike's cousin who lived in Perth. They also e-mailed the cousin and told him about us. He and his wife, Shirley, said they'd love to meet us. The two cousins had been corresponding because both had recently had open heart surgery to replace a heart valve. Sadly, about a month before we were to leave on the trip Mike's cousin in Perth passed away suddenly of a heart attack. Mike was quite upset at the news and worried that it might be a hereditary thing and he would be next. We felt it wouldn't be appropriate for us to make contact at this point and told Mike that we wouldn't. However, he thought that Shirley might still be interested in talking to us, so urged us to give her a call. The second week of our stay we called her. We planned to just talk to her and pass on best wishes from Mike and Joan, but instead she suggested we come one day for lunch. We set a date for later in the week. She said she lived in a rural area near the Swan River. It was rather complicated to find so we asked for the exact street address so we could put it in our GPS.

When we pulled into her yard, we knew we were in the right place as her dog, who came out to greet us was an exact duplicate of Joan and Mike's dog. Shirley was a delightful lady to talk to and we had a great visit as well as a delicious lunch. She lived on five acres on a river and had 14 pet kangaroos, although pet is probably a loose way of putting it as they were not fenced in and could go any time they wished. She said the males leave and come back whenever they want, but the females mainly stay close. Several of the females there that day had joeys in their pouches. Shirley and I hand fed them but she asked Doug to stand to one side for a while. Eventually she moved closer to Doug while still passing out food and finally stood right next to him. The kangaroos were a bit skittish at first but eventually a couple of the younger ones ate out of Doug's hand. She explained that they seldom saw men around, especially big ones like Doug, but some of the roos would let her two grandsons feed them. In addition to the dog and the kangaroos, she had chickens running around and a tiny new kitten.

She must have realized how her husband's passing had affected Mike because when we were sitting around talking after lunch, she told us of the circumstances of her husband's death and asked us to pass on to Mike that it was totally unrelated to the valve surgery and to make sure he understood that. We promised to do that. We left there feeling that we had made a new friend.

On the way back we passed the Margaret River Chocolate Company. I couldn't resist stopping but didn't buy anything. Somehow, $10.95 for a 100g chocolate bar that I can buy at home for $1.99 was too much for even this chocolate lover. Also, I like dark chocolate and most of theirs had stuff added – dark grape, dark brandy, dark chili (that last sounded horrible).

One day we decided it was time we marked another first; we had to see the Indian Ocean. Perth is not really on the ocean; it straddles the Swan River. Fremantle is the port of Perth and it is on the Indian Ocean about 14 kilometers downstream. The ocean beaches north of Fremantle are beautiful with miles and miles of white sand, but at the mouth of the Swan River is a deep-water container port. Fremantle was the site of the 1987 America's Cup race. Before that it was a typical port town, rundown and seedy. The government spruced it up before the Cup race and it is now a very trendy place to live with huge mansions along the waterfront and river between the two cities. We went on a tour that took us to Fremantle by bus and then back to Perth by boat on the Swan River. When we docked back in downtown Perth we took the CAT (Central Area Transit) back to the railway station where we caught the commuter train back to where we had left our car. One thing we found in most Australian cities was a free transit bus for tourists around the downtown area. It is such a good idea. We were able to see more, shop more, and visit more attractions using this bus than if we had to park our car every time.

While waiting for our train at the station we had a coffee and I had an iced coffee. I just love the Aussie iced coffees. They are so different from ours which are either insipid or so full of crushed ice they are difficult to suck through a straw. The iced coffee I got there is chilled but has no ice in it. They float a small lump of ice cream on top and swirl the whole thing with whipped cream, then sprinkle with shaved chocolate. I'd hate to guess the calorie count and probably don't want to know, but they sure were good.

The day after our Fremantle trip we took a drive to a place that Shirley recommended, Hillary's Boat Harbour. This is a marina about an hour's drive north of the city and has a magnificent beach. We left very early to beat the heat and the traffic, so stopped for breakfast at Gloria Jean's for their specialty of coffee and inch-thick buttered raisin toast. We got a seat on the edge of the dock where we could watch the boats and the children's safe beach. This beach is right next to the marina and inside the breakwater so the kids are protected from sharks, which grow pretty big and ferocious in the Indian Ocean. After walking the boardwalk for a while in the 37-degree heat and doing a little shopping, we decided to splurge on a seafood lunch at a restaurant called The Jetty. I don't remember what we had for lunch but we were impressed that they put a huge bottle of ice water on our table as soon as we sat down. Halfway through the meal when the bottle was empty, they replaced it with another and we drank the whole thing. In that heat we couldn't stop drinking water.

The next day we visited our first winery in the Swan River area. Chris and her husband, Greg, picked us up and we drove to

Sandalford Winery. The wines were quite good so we bought a bottle to take to a barbeque later that day. One interesting thing, the wine pourer in the tasting room, and his girlfriend who also worked there, were planning a visit to Canada later in the year, in our summer. Someone in their family had a piece of property with a cabin on it just outside Moncton, NB. When we said we knew the area they started asking us questions about things to do and see there and we were able to give them a list of must sees, such as Magnetic Hill, the Bay of Fundy and the Shediac Lobster Festival. And we also recommended that they drive the bridge to PEI. It was nice to give someone else travel information for a change.

The lunch was a bit of a shocker, obviously aimed at wine tourists and not locals. The main meals were priced in the mid $30s (and that was the lunch menu), so after a quick conference among the four of us, we each ordered a starter, still around $16, and a big bowl of fries to share. After we left the winery, we went to an ice cream shop for dessert. Then we went to Chris and Greg's house for lemonade and a quick tour of the house. Their home office was full of high-tech equipment as they did wedding videos and edited them into a wedding day story for the couple. Actually, Chris did most of the video work as Greg had another job and only did the videos on his day off. Greg also had an ultra-light plane and showed us some photos of the two-seater plane and the hanger he keeps it in. He said if we'd come a month or so later, he would have taken us up for a ride, but right then the airfield had a no-fly order. It's a grass runway, and as there had been no rain for about a month, it was tinder dry. Any sparks from the engine or even heat from the exhaust could start a bush fire. He couldn't fly again until they got a good rain.

We came home late in the afternoon and got ready to go to a barbecue.

Early that morning, Shirley, Mike's cousin's wife, called and said her daughter and husband and their two children were coming over for a barbecue and would we like to come. Of course, we said yes. The bottle of wine we'd bought earlier was a hostess gift. When we arrived at her house the kangaroos were all at the fence waiting to be fed, so we had another good look at them. We were only there a few minutes when the rest of the family arrived. The two boys, Shirley's grandsons, had been playing baseball earlier in the day and were avid baseball fans. This struck us as strange as cricket is usually the game of choice in Australia. We had a great barbecue dinner and afterwards I got out my laptop computer and pulled up some photos of Mike and Joan to show them. I also had some photos of our complex in Kelowna and could show them what our house looked like in the winter with snow piled up in the front yard. This intrigued the boys as they had never seen snow. Shirley's daughter was surprised at how much Mike looked like her father, but as they are cousins it was probably not surprising. They said they were planning a family trip to Canada in the next couple of years, and we said we hope to see them as we'd like to return their hospitality. However, they have never visited, so we haven't seen them since, although we exchanged Christmas cards with Shirley for several years.

Our last weekend in Perth we took the train into Fremantle to the Sunday Market. On the hour-long ride there were several stops and we enjoyed the signs posted on the crossings. They were typical blunt Aussie. There were different signs that all started with "Stay off the tracks". There were several different endings: "If you're lucky you'll only get hit with a $200 fine", "If you're still alive, it'll cost you $200.", " No matter what the odds are, the train always wins", "Your relatives won't have to scatter your remains, the train does a good job of that". You kind of got the idea you should stay off the tracks.

The last day of an exchange is usually a busy one. Besides our own packing, there is an understanding that you leave the place clean, towels and sheets laundered and the bed made. Also if you break anything you replace it and if you use up something in the fridge or cupboards, you replace it with the same or something else. In this place we knocked over and broke a ceramic paper towel rack. We couldn't find a replacement like it so bought a metal one. Not the same but at least it wouldn't break. We used up their salad dressing, jam and cookies, but left them a half-full 4-liter cask of red wine, so figured that was a good exchange. We also left them a new can of insect spray as we used up theirs on the fleas.

Chris and Greg came in their van to take us to the hotel where we spent the night before leaving on our two-day tour of the Margaret River wine area. We had a drink in the hotel lounge and then dinner. There was lots of talk and taking photos. They were a really nice couple and we hoped to keep in touch. Sometimes, as in this case, we never meet our exchange hosts, but become really good friends with their friends and neighbours.

The tour company office was only a block from our hotel, which we chose specifically because pickup time was 7:45 am. Margaret River is the premier winemaking area on Australia's west coast, and is a three-hour drive from Perth, which is why we wanted to use the tour company rather than drive ourselves.

Our first stop was Xanadu Winery, a really beautiful winery building. We liked some of their wines but didn't want to buy any wine this early in the trip. Next, we went to a raptor sanctuary where they had wedge-tailed eagles (we could have happily missed that one) and had lunch there. Lunch was a picnic lunch that the driver brought in coolers and set out on a tailgate.

Then we went to the highlight of the day, as far as I was concerned, Leeuwin Lighthouse. I love lighthouses anyway and am always photographing them, but this one was special. It is situated on the southwest corner of Australia, where the Indian Ocean and the Southern Ocean meet. Probably the next lighthouse in a southerly or westerly direction would be in India or Antarctica, thousands of miles away. There were very craggy rocks and very rough water, swirling every which way. It was also very windy walking around there. About the Southern Ocean – this was a name we had not encountered before. We thought this ocean south of Australia and New Zealand was the Antarctic Ocean, but everyone there called it the Southern Ocean and on maps it's listed as The Great Southern Ocean. We questioned it once and were told that well, yes, it is the Antarctic Ocean, but most people these days call it the Southern Ocean and the name just stuck and became common usage.

We stopped for the night at a place called Abby Beach Hotel, but there was no beach in sight. When we asked, we were told there was a beach but it was "a good walk" away. Since the definition of "a good walk" depends on who's saying it, we decided we didn't really need to see another beach.

Our first winery the next morning was a large one owned by a corporation. The wines tasted like they were made by a committee, very bland and not very good. Our years of living in the Okanagan with its excellent wineries have made us picky about the wine we buy. They did have some interesting t-shirts with a nice slogan, "Wine is sunshine mixed with water." I tried to buy one but they were so tiny that even the XL looked like it would fit a child.

The second winery was Redgate. They had some very good wines, including a Rose that was excellent, so we bought a bottle of that. We were told that Margaret River makes only 2% of Aussie wines but 25% of the premium wines. And we did taste some good ones. The last winery we went to was a small boutique winery owned by a real character, the type of person who could have been a stand-up comic. He had us laughing all the time. Someone asked how come his wife was listed on the sign as the winery manager, and he said it had to do with the license. A few years ago, when they brought in regulation in the wine industry, everyone who wanted a winery license, even those who had been in the business for many years, had to take a 3-day seminar and write an exam. He said that no way was anyone getting him in a classroom for three days, he already knew more about the business than they did. His wife, who had a cooler head (and probably a little more sense) took the seminar and wrote the exam and the winery license was issued in her name. So officially she's the boss. He had some really good wines. I liked a Semillon blend best. One different wine he had was one that his son made. It was a chili-infused Rose, made in mild or hot . Doug tasted the mild and it burnt his mouth, so we don't know what the hot was like. However, it was the most popular wine purchased by our group. Lastly, on the way back, we went to a cheese farm where we bought a small piece to take with us. We stayed at the same hotel we'd stayed at before and where we'd left our luggage. We only took a small carry bag on the bus tour.

After our two weeks in Perth, we would still have 11 days before our next exchange in Melbourne. Our travel agent, Annamarie, knew we liked trains and back home, when we were still planning our itinerary, she suggested we might like the Indian Pacific train across the Nullarbor Desert from Perth to Adelaide. We could stay in Adelaide for a week and then take an all-day train from Adelaide to Melbourne along the southern coast. We still had a couple of days to fill in, but we already knew we wanted to do a wine tour of the Margaret River, so figured we could make it work.

The Indian Pacific Train

The next morning, we started out on the next segment of our 2 ½ month journey, crossing the country on the Indian Pacific Railway. The train got its name because it travels all the way across Australia from the Indian Ocean to the Pacific. Although it goes all the way to Sydney, we were taking it only to Adelaide.

We checked our large bags and took only our carry bags with us. Here we had a momentary panic. Our ticket said we had cabin 15/16 in car J. The crew person checking us in said we were not on her manifest, someone else was in that cabin. She called over another member of the crew, who took our ticket back to the office to check the computer. She brought back our ticket with a new car and number written across it. We had been relocated, probably because a group booking wanted to be close together. We were told that this train was a lot longer than usual and that extra cars had been added, including some older cars from the Ghan Train that goes north to Darwin. Unfortunately, we got one of the older cars in our reallocation. What was good was that the beds were longer than the beds on the Canadian Via Rail and Doug fit with no problem. There was a private bathroom in our cabin and it was the most unusual we've ever seen. Stepping into it was like stepping into a shower stall, smooth walls with a shower head. There was a handle on the wall on one side that when pulled down opened up into a toilet seat. You pulled it down to use it and folded it back up to flush. A handle set into the opposite wall was a pull-down basin with taps that didn't stay on. They only worked as long as you held them. To empty the basin, you simply folded it back into the wall. Set into the wall above the basin was a mirror. You could actually sit on the toilet and wash your face at the same time. We later discovered that when the train was travelling at high speed it was sometimes safer to do just that. Neat, but weird.

During the trip over the next three days, we met a lot of very interesting people, both at meals in the dining room and sitting around the lounge car. We only met one other Canadian couple on the train, and they were from Saskatchewan. We talked to a few people from the UK, but most of the passengers were Aussies. For some of them it was their 5th or 6th time on the train. One couple we talked to stayed in Perth only two days and took the next train back. The train journey both ways was their holiday, much like we do with cruise ships.

The only complaint we had was the food. The railway's advertising mentioned their gourmet food and we had heard from others that the food on the train was great. Well, we may have been spoiled by the food on Canada's Via Rail, but we were not impressed by the Indian Pacific's meals. In our opinion it was no better than camp food.

Our first night on the train we were warned not to go to bed early as there was a special treat at a late-night stop. We arrived in Kalgoorlie, a gold mining town about 10 pm. When we got off the train there were buses lined up to show us the town in the dark. Kalgoorlie was the site of a gold rush in the late 1800s and some of the buildings date from then, much like our Dawson City in the Klondike. I would have loved to see some of them in the light. We were taken to the Super Pit, an open pit gold mine, 3 ½ km wide and almost 1 km deep. The trucks on the bottom looked like dinky toys, although we were told they were monsters that cost $4 million each. There was a shovel from one of the diggers sitting at the top of the pit and I took Doug's photo standing in it. The shovel was twice as high as Doug. I spent most of my time at the pit head giving photography lessons. People were taking pictures using flash and getting nothing but a few pinpricks of light. I was telling them to turn off their flash, brace the camera on the railing and take a time exposure. The difference was amazing. The pit was well lit, and doing it that way they got lots of detail.

After leaving the gold mine we got another surprise. We were taken by bus along the main street, which turned out to be a red-light district. The buildings were like store fronts and most were occupied by scantily-clad girls who stood at their windows and smiled and waved at us as we drove slowly by. They obviously knew we were from the train and were determined to give us a show that we could talk about later. We were surprised that prostitution was actually legal here, the only place in Australia where it is.

The other thing that surprised us is that the huge trucks in the pit and some of the other heavy equipment are driven by women as often as men. Our bus driver was tiny, barely five feet tall, and we wondered if she could handle the bus until she told us she used to be a truck driver in the mine. She drove the tour bus now because she got tired of working shifts. The funny thing is that she didn't like working the night shift and here she was driving the tour bus at midnight.

It was well after midnight before we got to bed, but the bunks were surprisingly comfortable so we got a good night's sleep. By morning we were well into the Nullarbor Plain, or Nullarbor Desert as it's called on some maps. If you want to see flat red earth and nothing for miles, this was the place to see it. At first, we saw a few trees and cows with the occasional ranch or station. Then even those disappeared and there was only sand and scrub as far as we could see on the horizon. During the night and into the morning we were on the straightest piece of track in the world, 600 miles without a bend. Around noon we got a chance to get off the train again, at a stop called Cook. I wouldn't call it a town as it only has 12 inhabitants. We were there for about an hour as the train was refueled and took on water. We got off and walked around but it was so hot and dusty that we didn't last long, It was in the middle of the desert with no vegetation and no shade. Although the town was officially called Cook, its unofficial name was The Middle Of Nowhere, and there was a big hand painted sign that said that.

Earlier that day we saw the first sign of life outside, a couple of kangaroos bounding across the desert in the distance. Some people said they saw some wild camels, but that was earlier before we got up.

Our last day on the train was very uneventful. It rained off and, on all day, and we saw a lot of rainbows in the distance. It was a great day just to sit around and talk to our fellow passengers and that's what we did.

The train arrived in Adelaide about 7am, much too early to check into our hotel, so we left our bags at the hotel and went in search of some coffee.

Our favourite hotel in Adelaide was fully booked as this was still the summer holiday season, so we had booked this one on the internet. We knew it was undergoing renovations, but the website said that only refurbished rooms were being rented. It was billed as a 4-star hotel with the regular rate $280 reduced to $110 during renovations. We figured we could put up with a little noise for that rate. When we got to our room it definitely had not been refurbished. The bathroom was OK, but the bed was soft and saggy and the furniture was old and smelled musty, I called the front desk and complained and the girl said, "But the bathroom has been done over. I replied that the website when we booked specifically said "refurbished rooms only would be rented" and the bed was totally unacceptable. The result was that we got another room on another floor and it was a very nice room with all new furniture including a couch and a refrigerator. So, it pays to complain. Of course, I had to do the complaining. Doug says that's my job as I'm so much better at it than he is - which is true.

The broadband also wasn't working during renovations so we went next door to another hotel and found out they have free wireless in their lobby, so that's where we went the next morning for breakfast. We went to an Italian restaurant nearby for dinner and found out that they also had free wifi. It was great that we didn't have any problem getting our e-mail.

The next day was Australia Day, their national holiday, a holiday that we've spent in Australia several times now. We took the tram to Victoria Square and found a place to sit to enjoy the parade. In the lead was a bagpipe band, which made us feel right at home. There were a lot of service clubs and groups as well as a vintage car club. But what really surprised us was the huge number of ethnic communities represented. From a small group of six from Eritrea, to a huge group from Viet Nam with dancers, a band and a lot of people just walking in native dress. The most fun group was from Tonga. They were on a flatbed truck with a band, singing and dancing. There were also Aboriginal dancers on another flatbed. After eating a snag for lunch (a sausage to all you non-Aussies), we went back to our hotel, stopping at a supermarket to buy drinks, coke, Gatorade and iced coffee. As long as it was liquid, we needed it. We found that there in the heat we drank a lot and it was probably the largest part of our food budget. We were also drinking sports drinks, which we hardly ever do at home, because we needed the electrolytes.

We stopped at a Tourist Info Centre and booked a couple of events, a wine tour of the Barossa Valley and tickets to the show Miss Saigon, as we had missed it when it played back home in Kelowna the previous year. Later we went to the Italian restaurant again, bought a cola and sat there for half an hour picking up e-mail and updating our blog. Free wifi they promised and free it was, so we had dinner there again for a second night.

The next thing on our agenda in Adelaide was dealing with a camera problem. We'd been getting a fuzzy black spot in the center of all our pictures recently. I thought it might be dirt on the lens so took the lens off as well as the filter and cleaned both. However, the next picture still had the blob, so we had to go to a camera store. The girl behind the counter asked a few questions and said it might be a speck of dust inside the camera body. She took it apart and gave it a couple of blasts of air from a pressure can, and sure enough the spot was gone. Whew, that was a relief! We were only a third of the way through our Aussie trip, so would have been very unhappy to have a useless camera.

On our second last day in Adelaide, we went on a wine tour to the Barossa Valley. We had gone two years before with Keith and Ann and had a great time so thought we'd go again. It was billed as the Supreme Barossa Experience, with five wineries, all good, all different. The first one was Wolf Blass, the only one we'd been to before. We tasted several wines, most very good, and bought one. The last time we were here we bought a Port and we'd planned to buy another, but found this year's offerings rather insipid. This was the largest winery on today's itinerary. The second one was Maggie Beer's Farm Shop & Winery The winery was actually called Beer Brothers – a strange name for a winery, Apparently Maggie Beer was a TV celebrity cook, who was known as a local character. She did cooking demos at the winery a couple of times a week, but not that day. There was quite a large store attached to the winery with Maggie Beer products, stuff like pheasant pate, chili salsa and onion jam. The wines were so-so. The next one, Barossa Valley Estate Winery, was probably the most beautifully modern building, all glass and stone. We both liked some of the wines but were not interested in buying any. We had a delicious lunch at this winery, a selection of breads, sliced meats and cheeses, including a glass of wine. I had a Rose, which was really being pushed that year after being ignored for many years. The only thing we bought here was a chocolate bar that had raisins infused with Shiraz. It sounded interesting.

The fourth winery, Langmeil Estate was the most interesting, and the oldest. We were taken on a vineyard tour and shown vines that were the oldest in the world at 160 years. Apparently, vineyards in other parts of the world were wiped out at some time by a root fungus, but not here. Some of those vines were about 8 inches in diameter and all twisted and gnarled - quite interesting. I didn't go on the last portion of the tour so I started talking to the retail person in the winery. He had been to a couple of international conferences and knew about the Okanagan. He was asking me about ice wines and I asked him about late harvests, as most of the wineries seem to have them, despite the lack of frost. He said that most of their late harvests are done with grapes from vines that have the botrytis fungus. I can't imagine wine with that fungus tasting as a good as some of their late harvests do. This winery had the best wines and we bought two bottles, a really special white and a 10-year-old Port that was the best we had tasted on this trip.

The last winery was Chateau Tarunda, an elegant place that looked like a castle. When I first saw it, I said it was the same design as the City Hall in Frankfurt, Germany, and when I asked, I was told that it was built by the original German owners, but they no longer owned it. By this time my head was swirling and I only tasted one, a Semillon blend. Doug tasted several, including a couple if wines in the $100 range, but we didn't buy any here as we had as many as we needed or could carry. I should say here that the tastings are not measured, some of them are just slopped in the glass and are much larger than the pourings we get back home. I fell asleep on the 1 ½ hour ride back, and I suspect a few others did as well. The whole tour was interesting and as it was only a small group of 10 persons, we got to know each other. There were two other Canadians on the bus, an aunt and niece from Victoria and Richmond, BC.

Our last day in Adelaide we had booked a matinee performance of Miss Saigon at the Festival City Theatre. This was one of the nicest theatres we had ever been in. It was beautiful, all glass with terraces off both the first and balcony floors. It was just as good inside, with large comfortable seats and lots of leg room. We were in two seats on the aisle and we didn't even have to stand up when people walked past us to get to their seats. We were amused at the clientele, however, and Doug commented that the matinee must be when the aged and the disabled go. The foyer was lined with walkers and wheelchairs. The people all around us knew each other, so we guessed they must have been driven from some retirement community like ours at home. We fitted right in. The show was fantastic, the staging and the effects were great. What surprised us was that the show had no dialogue, it was totally sung, like an opera.

Right now, I have to give a 'shout out' to McDonald's. I know some people poke fun at McDonald's, but it really is the traveller's friend. In Australia it was one of the few places you could find a restroom, and the only place we could find North American style coffee. Everyone here drinks espresso, lattes or that strong horrible instant stuff with the brown foam on top. But back to the restrooms - the streets were lined with coffee shops, ice cream shops and restaurants of all kinds and none of them had an on-site restroom. At home, that is a requirement of being in the food business. I think most of the bars have them, as for them it really is a necessity if they want to keep their patrons for multiple drinks. But at most of the little restaurants and coffee shops, when we asked, they would tell us there was a public toilet about two blocks away, or they would recommend we go to one of the big department stores like Myers. The food court in the mall didn't even have one; we had to go out of the food court to the back of the mall behind the escalators and down a long hallway. As you can possibly tell, we'd been caught a few times in desperate need and you can't believe how welcome a sight those golden arches were. When we were far from home it was like meeting an old friend.

We finally realized on the last day while packing that my favourite sunhat was missing. I hadn't seen it since the Indian Pacific train. I called the railway station and asked for Lost and Found. And guess what!. They actually had it. I had to describe it, down to the maple leaf pin stuck in it, but they had it and it was waiting for me at the sales desk when we went there in the morning to board the Overlander train for Melbourne.

We do love travelling on trains in Australia and this one was no exception. Since this wasn't a long-distance train there was no dining room, but they did have a food car where you could pick up food and bring it back to your seat. The seats had fold down trays, much like airline seats.

It was interesting to see the landscape change as we went inland and south, from the lush vineyards around Adelaide to brown scrub with cattle and sheep further south. It was quite desert-like in the interior and we even saw a couple of salt flats and dry river beds. As we got closer to Melbourne it changed again to a green and treed landscape. The last half hour into the city we could get glimpses of the ocean and of the city in the distance. It looked like we were going around a bay.

Our exchange home was in a suburb of Melbourne called Williamstown and we arrived there about 7:30 pm, seeing for the first time our home for the next month. It was a white bungalow, tucked away from the street behind a front courtyard with a stone fence and a white wrought iron gate across the driveway. It looked very pretty from the outside. Inside it was much bigger than it looked from the outside, with tiled floors throughout and a nice well-equipped kitchen. We knew right away we would enjoy our stay here. With no available groceries and not much in the fridge as our hosts had been gone for over a week, we opted to go to the pub about two blocks away for dinner. However, we forgot about it being Friday night, which is Aussie party night for the younger ones, and for the older working blokes on Friday night it's a tradition to have a beer after work with your workmates. The pub was full and the crowd spilled out into the street. Doug pushed his way in and asked about dinner, but it was over an hour wait. We walked back home, found some bread in the freezer and had eggs on toast, the only thing we could find resembling a meal.

The next morning, we had no choice but to brave the Saturday morning crowds at the supermarket, and I do mean brave, starting in our own driveway. The house was set far back from the road and that meant backing the car down a long driveway and out between the gates into heavy traffic. Doug is still not great with backing a car while sitting on the right side. In figuring out where the back of the car is your judgement is skewed. Then I had to stand out on the road edge and tell him when there was no traffic, as he had to back directly into a traffic lane. Lastly, I had to get myself into the car before more traffic came. We decided right then that we would always approach it from the direction that had us on the curb side so we could back into the driveway.

As well as stocking up on groceries, we also had to get some wine. We do love Aussie wine, especially the price. This time we bought two 4-liter boxes from Di Bartolo, the winner of Winery of the Year. The wines we bought were a Traminer Reisling blend for me and a Cabernet Merlot for Doug, both were $16 for the box and were excellent wines.

When we got back from shopping, we got a phone call from a friend of our hosts who asked how we were doing and asked us for dinner later in the week. Here, as in most places, we got to meet the friends of our hosts and often became friends with them.

Early the next week we made our first trip to downtown Melbourne. As we were in a suburb and Melbourne is a big city, we decided to use the transit system whenever we went into the city. The train station was about a 10-minute walk from our house, although long-legged Doug said he could walk it in only 5 minutes if he didn't have to slow down for me. For seniors, the price was $3.40 for an all-day ticket that we could use on trains, buses or trams. It took us right into Flinders Station in the downtown. From there we could get either the free bus or the tram to anywhere in the CBD or Central Business District. We could travel on any bus we like, but chose the free one as it's the one most tourists use as it had a commentary along the way. The first one we chose was filled with a Japanese tour group with a guide, which we thought was a bit cheap of the tour company if they were charging them for a tour of the city. They were all talking among themselves and no one was listening to the guide, and the cacophony of voices was ear-splitting so we couldn't hear the commentary, so we got off at the next stop and started walking. We were looking for a RACV store, Royal Automobile Club of Victoria, the equivalent of our CAA or the USA's AAA, to get a couple of maps. Unfortunately, they're not free like our BCAA maps, so we bought the one we wanted most, as well as a waist purse with a holder for a water bottle, a necessity in that heat. We also picked up some brochures, one of them for a day tour of the Great Ocean Road. Everyone said we had to see this area, but driving a hilly, curving coastal road was not something we wanted to do right then. We'd be too busy keeping the car on the road to do much sightseeing.

One thing we wanted to do while in Melbourne was to go on a tour to Tasmania. We had hoped to pick up a 3 or 4 day tour, but most tours were 10 or 12 days with a couple at 7 days, but none shorter than that. So, we scrapped that idea. Tasmania would have to wait for another time.

One day on a trip to the supermarket I visited the restroom and it was the most automated I have ever used. It did everything but wipe your bum. It was so interesting I absolutely had to write about it. From the outside it looked like an elevator, with a metal door. A green button set into the door edge read "vacant" and a red button said "engaged". The green button was lit so I pressed it. The metal door slid open like something in Star Wars. I stepped inside and a voice said, "Press the green button and the door will close and lock". I did, and it did. The toilet paper dispenser looked empty, there was nothing hanging out of it, but there was a black button on top. I pressed the button and it spat out three sheets. They looked a bit skimpy so I pressed it again and got three more sheets. A third press produced nothing so I guess I got my allotment. When I was done, I looked around to flush but there was no handle, so I went to wash my hands at a long skinny trough set into the wall. It was marked: Soap – Water – Dry, and underneath was a sign that read, "Washing hands will flush toilet". That sounded interesting so I stuck my hands under Soap, and sure enough a blob of soap dropped. Then I put my hands under Water and, as well as getting water to wash my hands the toilet magically flushed. Then sticking my hands under Dry, I got dried. Then all that was left was getting out of this little metal prison. The green button I had pressed to close the door had a sign that read "Press to Open". I did, and it did. Thank goodness! One other thing, after the door closed and locked the voice said, "You have 10 minutes. If you have not exited in that time the door will automatically open". My whole time in there I had visions of not being finished in time and being caught bare assed in public when the door opened.

I've mentioned before about the information binder that every-one leaves for their exchangers. Every one is different, because every house has unique circumstances. This one mentioned the drought conditions in the area and what to do about it. The number one rule there is that every drop of water is precious and not to waste any of it. We found a plastic bucket with a carry handle in the shower. This was to catch the water when you first turn on the taps and have to wait for the water to warm up enough to shower. Usually that first blast of cold water goes down the drain; here you catch it and save it for watering the indoor plants. When washing fruits and vegetables before eating or putting away in the fridge, we were asked to put a dishpan in the sink to catch the water and use that as well as any other relatively clean water (no soapy water) to water outside plants. Also, outside plants should not be watered in the heat of the day, only before 8 am or after 8 pm. There was also a rain barrel in the backyard to catch roof runoff if it rained. This could also be used to water plants. There was no sprinkler system and no lawn grass; the front yard was landscaped with plants set in rock beds.

The day we toured the Great Ocean Road was a beautiful day and a great experience. We had been told it was something we had to do, but we really didn't know the story behind it or what it was all about. The company we chose used a Mercedes 10-seater van, so we knew the tour group was small. We knew from experience in other places that a small tour group was so much better than the huge 50 seat buses used by some. Our driver was named Grace and we met up along the way with a second van driven by her husband, Brian. That's when we found out it was a small family-owned business. It was about a 2-hour ride to the start of the coastal road and we stopped along the way for morning tea. This wasn't a formal tea in a restaurant but a real Aussie "billy tea" at a roadside park. We walked down to look at the beach and the soaring cliffs on either side while Grace and Brian set out the tea mugs, crackers with Vegemite, and Lamingtons. They waited until we got back to make the tea as it was part of the show. Billy tea is tea made in a tin can or pot boiled over an open fire. However, they brought hot water in thermoses and poured it over the tea in a tin pail with a handle. When the tea had steeped for a few minutes, Grace took it away from the picnic table to an open part of the field and swung it in a circle over her head five times without spilling a drop. She said it was to use centrifugal force to settle the tea leaves to the bottom. We enjoyed our tea and snack. Vegemite, which the Aussies use like we do peanut butter, is made from the yeast leavings of making beer. It's supposed to be very high in vitamins, but is an acquired taste. Despite several winters in Australia, we have yet to acquire a taste for vegemite. And Lamingtons are squares of pound cake, covered in chocolate and sprinkled with coconut. It was named for a former Australian governor who liked his cake dipped that way. They're an Aussie institution and you'll find them for sale in bulk packages in the supermarket as well as individually in the coffee shops.

Our second stop was to see some koalas in the wild. There are lots of koalas in wildlife parks but seeing them in the wild is rare. We saw three, two of them sleeping and the other eating. We learned that eating and sleeping is about all they do, sometimes sleeping up to 20 hours a day. We also visited a tropical rainforest to see one of Australia's largest trees, and another stop for lunch.

Shortly after lunch we arrived at the Twelve Apostles. The Apostles are the big event on this road, named for the twelve large stone spires sticking up out of the ocean. But when we saw them there were only eleven as one had collapsed the previous year. This was in 2009, and when a friend visited the area three years later two more of them had collapsed. So it looks as if a big tourist attraction will soon be a big bust. It will still be a popular drive, however, as the curving, hilly coastal road is quite spectacular.

The interpretation centre was on top of a steep cliff overlooking the ocean and beach below. From the beach you could get quite close to some of the stone spires, but as it was 176 steps down the cliff face to the beach we opted to stay at the top. From the cliff top we could see all eleven of the standing stones so we got some good photos. A little further along there was another rock formation of sea stacks, high flat stacks of rock, looking like boards standing on end. A couple had holes in them, making arches. One arch, called London bridge, looked just like The Arches on the northern peninsula of Newfoundland. After all this ocean and rock viewing, we went to another small town for a light supper of soup and bread, and then the three-hour trip back to the city. We arrived back after 9 pm; a very long but very interesting day.

The day after our Ocean Road tour, our host's friends, Mel and Margaret, called and invited us to lunch. They live in an older part of Melbourne known as Albert Park. This is an area of old Victorian and Edwardian homes that have all been restored and modernized. We had a delicious lunch and sat and talked for hours. They were travellers as well, but not home exchangers.

One of our previous exchange couples, Val and Lyle, who owned the condo at Magic Mountain on the Gold Coast, live in Ballarat, a gold mining town about 50 miles north of Melbourne. We had met them when they came to our place and also met them for lunch in Stockholm, Sweden, when they were there on an exchange and we were on a cruise. We had kept in touch by e-mail and felt like old friends. When they heard we were staying in Melbourne for a month they invited us to come visit them in Ballarat for a few days. We didn't want to drive that distance so they suggested we take the interstate train that stops in Ballarat. The train trip was about an hour and a half and Val and Lyle met us at the station. After lunch Lyle took us on a tour of the area. First, we went to the Wildlife Park to see some of Australia's famous kangaroos and koalas, as well as echidnas and goannas. We didn't see any wombats or Tasmanian devils as they were inside out of the heat. After that he took us to the Eureka stockade where the gold miners revolted against the government about the charging of license fees for mining gold, and changed the face of Australian government, leading to it becoming a free country instead of being governed by the British. It was the Aussie equivalent of the Boston Tea Party. Val stayed home and cooked dinner as they had invited another couple for dinner. They lived just two doors away and are, like most Aussies we met, a delightful couple. The dinner conversation went on for hours.

The next day we went off by ourselves to Sovereign Hill, a theme park about mining. Val and Lyle had been here many times, so just dropped us off at the gate. We had a very interesting and tiring day. Sovereign Hill is much like Barkerville in BC, with all the old buildings dating from the gold rush days and people dressed up in period costume re-enacting events. There was even a school class there, dressed in period costumes. One of the stores sold copies of clothes or household items that were used in those days. There were two mine tours, one shallow and the other quite deep. They have demos of pouring pure molten gold into molds and of soldiers drilling and firing muskets. We also went for a ride in a stagecoach, and later tried our hand at panning for gold in a stream. We went across the street to the Gold Museum that told all about the gold rush in the area. There was even a life-size copy of the largest nugget ever found. I bought a couple things in the gift shop, including a vial of gold flakes, so I came back home with some Aussie gold.

We were enjoying this visit so much that when Val and Lyle asked if we'd like to stay another day and meet some more of their friends, we happily agreed. First, they took us to see some of the Grampion Range of mountains. They were impressive in an otherwise flat landscape, but were really only small hills to us who live near the Rockies. Then we visited their friends John and Glenda for morning tea. John showed us the house where he grew up, which was just around the corner from the house where John and Glenda lived when they were first married and for many years after. And they were both just down the street from where they now live. So in 70+ years John has moved a total of 1 ½ blocks. Quite a contrast from our history of six provinces, one state and 15 houses or apartments. Lyle wanted to take us to a place called The Hills, but we had to turn back as the road was closed due to a bush fire. Then Val and Lyle showed us where they grew up and their first house. They are retired motel owners and they showed us their first three motels as well as the motel they still own and lease out.

One sad thing we saw as we toured around was dried up lakes. They've been in a drought situation for close to 10 years and gradually all the lakes have disappeared. One lake, right in Ballarat, used to be 7 km around. Now it is gone. There were a couple of rowing clubs on the edge, but they were now shuttered with their jetties high and dry with grass growing up all around. A sailing club was the same. Several lakeshore restaurants that used to have decks over the water, now had nothing but brown grass to look out on. The same went for dozens of lakefront homes. Where once they had beautiful views of lake with birds and sailboats, they now looked out on brown dried out grass. It was definitely not the time to sell hoping for a good price. Down at the end of the lake was a slimy wet patch about 20 feet across, the last remnants of what was once a lovely recreational area within the town.

When we got back to our Williamstown after our trip to Ballarat, we went to see a travel agent to discuss the trip to Tasmania again. We saw a good price advertised in the paper but it was not for this time of year and not on short notice. Most of the hotels were full.

February in Australia is like our September, when the kids go back to school the seniors start travelling. So Tasmania bit the dust again.

One day we decided to drive to the town of Werribee, about 30 km away, because they had a large regional shopping center and we wanted something specific that we couldn't find in Williamstown. We wouldn't give a thought to such a short trip back home; we'd just get in the car and go. But there we had to plot it out on the map, noting roads and exits along the way. Even then we got off the highway an exit too soon and had to drive in a circle to get back on to get where we were going. One thing we noticed in the smaller towns was the lack of street signs. They were either not signed at all or the sign was very small and perched on top of several other signs. With the latter, by the time you figure out which sign is the correct one, you're past the street anyway. I guess if you lived in the town you wouldn't need street signs so it wasn't a huge priority. But when you're lost you need to know where you are before you can get where you're going. I consider myself a good map reader and navigator, but when you arrive at a major intersection with lights or a round-about, and none of the four streets leading into it has a name sign, even the best map is useless. We did eventually find the shopping mall and bought what we were looking for, so it was a successful if frustrating trip.

We've mentioned several times how impressed we were with the train systems in Australia. One day when we were on our way home after spending a couple of hours in a shopping mall on the second floor of a train station, we were marvelling at how complex the system was and yet how seamlessly the long-distance trains meshed with the local ones. We were at a major station, Southern Cross, which had 14 platforms and trains were coming and going on most of them. In the 15 minutes we waited for our train out to Williamstown, five other trains stopped at our platform alone. There were city loop trains, suburban trains like ours, and interstate trains like the one we used to go to Ballarat earlier in the week. And when we arrived in Melbourne two weeks before, we came on a train from Adelaide that stopped at this station. There was also a train that went to Canberra and Sydney. In addition to all these trains, the city was served by buses and trams on the streets. And any of these trains, trams or buses could be accessed with one ticket. A one-way ticket was $2.10, cheaper if you bought a strip, and was good for travel anywhere for two hours from when you first used it. A seniors' daily ticket for $3.50 was good for all day on any transport and could be used until midnight. Melbourne is about the same size as Vancouver, but Vancouver's transit can't touch Melbourne's.

Another thing we loved there was the markets. Sunday was market day and there was one in Williamstown where we could get local produce. There was also one downtown at the Arts Center where they had a craft market every Sunday. These were really nice things, paintings, silk scarves, aboriginal crafts, etc. There were so many things I'd love to have bought but I already had more than I could fit in my luggage.

One Sunday when we got back there was an e-mail from our friends in Brisbane, whom we had exchanged with several years ago, confirming they were coming to Melbourne for a visit and giving us the name and address of their hotel. We were anxious to see them and meet their new addition, baby Daniel, who was only a few months old.

Once we got used to the transit system and weren't always anxiously looking for our next stop, we could look around and enjoy the sights from the bus. We were really amazed by the architecture in Melbourne. The museum was a fabulous building, all angles and slanted sides and glass. So was the arts centre with its center spire that looks like the Eiffel Tower. The tallest building in the city was an 88-floor residential building with a glass-floored observation deck jutting out of the 88th floor. Can you imagine looking between your feet at the ground over a thousand feet below?

About three weeks into our one month stay we woke up one morning to rain. RAIN! This was the first time we'd seen rain since we'd been there and, by the excitement of the TV weatherman, the first it had rained in a long time. That helped the garden as the rain barrel was getting rather low. With it raining it was a good day to go shopping, as we needed another suitcase. No surprise here as we do this all the time. Our basement at home is full of odds and ends of cheap suitcases bought on trips when we shopped too much. We added another one to put into next spring's garage sale back home.

When it was still raining the next day, we decided to go to the casino. We're not gamblers, but we occasionally go to casinos because the food is usually good and inexpensive. We played the slot machines for a while before lunch and were both up a few dollars. After lunch we went back to the machines and what we had won before was lost very quickly. A guy sitting next to us told us it was no good to play in the afternoon as all the seniors were there, the place was full and the machines weren't paying. He said it's best to play very early or at night. I think that was very mean of the casinos to take the seniors' money like that with such a poor payout.

There was one interesting sidelight that had nothing to do with the casino. I sometimes like to people-watch in different places and sometimes pick up characters that I can incorporate in stories I write. I saw one at the casino's lunch buffet. A couple sat down at the table next to us. He was a big guy who started to talk to his companion as soon as he sat down. As he wasn't speaking English, I tuned him out, but still was aware of him as his voice was very loud. He went to the buffet and came back with his plate heaped. He started to talk again as soon as he sat down in a very rapid-fire sort of way and also took two phone calls. I thought to myself that if he didn't stop talking and eat, all that food was going to get cold, but when I looked at his plate it was half empty. Then I watched in fascination as he kept talking non-stop, very fast and very loud, and every scrap of food disappeared, down to sucking the chicken bones clean. All without choking or even without spraying food across the table. I still can't figure out how he could chew and swallow and talk and breathe all at the same time, fast and non-stop. It was obvious that he'd had a lot of practice. His wife hardly said a word other than "Uh huh" a few times, and it took her longer to eat less than half the food he ate while he talked continuously. Interesting character, although not one I would like to spend any time with.

Early in the morning of the day we went to the casino, the latest Cunard ship, the Queen Victoria, sailed into Melbourne and her docking was on the TV news as it was her maiden voyage. Our train went near the water as we came home and we tried to see her but couldn't. As she left that night just after dark, she was serenaded with fireworks from shore and answered with much horn blowing. As the forecast for that night and the next day was for showers and strong winds, they probably had a rough ride to Sydney.

The next day we had company for dinner, the first time we cooked dinner for someone else on this trip. Doug and Terry from Brisbane arrived with little Daniel in a stroller. Daniel was a real surprise when they first told us about him. We've known them for a few years, ever since we exchanged with them in Brisbane. They were in their mid-40's, in a second marriage and settled in careers, so we never expected this news. Terry said he was a surprise to them as well. They said he hadn't stopped them travelling as this is the second trip they'd been on and he wasn't even 4 months old yet. Doug is a real hands-on father, feeding and changing the baby. I made a real Canadian meal, my chicken and sausage casserole in BBQ sauce, with mashed potatoes and carrots and chocolate cake for dessert. No shrimp on the barbie!

The next day we met them downtown for lunch and they took us to a hotel bar that had a famous nude painting hanging over the bar. The bar was called Chloe's and the painting is of a woman named Chloe. It was part of an art exhibit back in the early 1900s when Melbourne hosted the World's Fair. Some of the paintings exhibited were sold to local people including this nude. People back then were scandalized when it was hung in public in the bar, but it's been there for almost a hundred years.

We had a couple of stops to make on the way back home as our time in Melbourne was getting short. We needed to go to a bank for some New Zealand money as our third exchange on this trip was in that country. Also we both needed some new books. We read a lot and we were running out. We knew we would find a Salvo (Aussie slang for Salvation Army) thrift store on the way back. We were able to buy several for 50 cents each, which certainly beats the $18 or $20 charged for new paperbacks in the stores. One sad note at the Salvo, they had a table covered with dolls with porcelain heads and all dressed in silk and velvet gowns. They were selling for $20 each and the lady in the store said they had just come in from an estate. They were beautiful and I can just imagine some lady collecting these for many years. At that price they would not last long. And, no, I didn't buy one. I had to remember suitcase space.

Our last weekend we went to a Wine & Food Festival. There was an open-air market and demo area on the terrace along the river downtown. The theme of this market was Slow Food (in contrast to Fast Food) and most of the booths were doing demos on and selling organic products. We tried a few things but weren't really interested in purchasing. The brownies made with Belgian chocolate were sinfully good, but at $4 per brownie or $39 per dozen, we passed. I promised Doug I would make him a batch of my cream cheese brownies when we got home.

Walking to the train to go back home we saw a store called High and Mighty, that carries big and tall clothes. Doug wanted to check it out so we went in and he bought a nice pair of cargo shorts.

Most of the time our scheduling went really well, but we had a glitch-filled morning here in Melbourne that almost resulted in missing our flight. One problem is bad enough when you have a flight to catch, but we had three that morning.

We had a taxi scheduled to pick us up at 8 am. We were out by the sidewalk with all our bags by 8. We didn't want to lock the door before our car arrived, just in case. Well, just in case happened. When no one had turned up by 8:10 Doug went back in to call. The phone rang just as he went in and it was the driver. There was no one at the address he had been given. We were at ## Melbourne Rd in Williamstown, and he'd been given ## Williamstown Rd in Melbourne. He eventually got there and we got to the airport.

As we were travelling business class, check-in was no problem. However, Immigration & Security was a problem. In Australia you have to go through a check on the way out, as they require a visa to let you in and they want to make sure you've left. My passport didn't scan and I had to go to a second security point for a further check. The reason it didn't scan was because I got it wet once (Doug spilled a drink on it in a motel.) But that was two years ago and I went through Europe the previous summer with no problem. Only in Australia was it a problem. I was finally cleared, but the girl in security said I would need a new passport before entering Australia again, meaning they wouldn't let me in with my wrinkled passport.

Then going through the security process, as my carry-on bag went through the

X-ray they said I had scissors in my bag. I knew I didn't pack scissors, but they insisted, so I took everything out of the bag and there were no scissors. They put the empty bag through and there were the scissors. They even showed me on the X-ray and I had to agree. So we went looking again and found them in the outside pocket poked through a hole in the lining so they weren't visible by just looking. Then the security guy gave me the two plastic boxes we'd put stuff in and I had to repack the bag. I wasn't sure I had everything, but they said I did. Then, when we were waiting to board the plane and they were calling our flight, there was an announcement on the speaker about keys left behind in security. I had keys in my bag, so I checked and not only were they missing but so was the plastic accordion folder with all our confirmations and documentation for the rest of the trip. I ran back to security, collared some guy and insisted they look for my folder and keys. They found another plastic box with all my stuff in it right by the X-ray machine. Apparently, they had taken it out of the pocket while looking for the scissors. So I grabbed them and ran (yes ran) all the way back to the gate. Luckily it was a huge 747 and they were still loading. The rest of the experience was pretty good. We were flying Air New Zealand and this was the first time we'd flown business or first class in a airline with the new flat bed seats. Instead of being two and two, the seats were all single, like little suites. I could see out the window by looking over my shoulder, but there was a wall between Doug and me. There was a space behind my seat with a pillow and a blanket. This is only a

3-hour flight, but I thought that if this is what I was going to have flying home overnight from New Zealand in three weeks, it would be a pleasure.

It took us a while to get through customs in Auckland. We had brought some food with us from the last place, tea, coffee, peanut butter, cheese, etc. Since NZ is very strict on what can be brought into the country, we declared it so as not to get into trouble. After reading the restrictions we were sure we would lose some of it. But after sending us to the wrong place, X-raying all our luggage, big and small, we walked out with everything, even the cheese. It was a big hassle over nothing. A shuttle picked us up and drove us into Hamilton to meet our exchange people. We were staying in their house in Hamilton and driving to their vacation house in Lake Taupo the next day. Whew, what a day! We were wrung out mentally and physically. A funny thing happened to end our stressful day. I was hot and sweaty and really needed a shower before bed. That's when I discovered that the bathroom had no door into the bedroom, just an archway, and the whole room was surrounded by windows. I could sit on the toilet and look across the yard and at the cows in the field. I wasn't worried about the cows, but neighbours were something else. We were on top of a hill so I guess they figured that had complete privacy and never closed the drapes. But I wasn't going to stand in a lighted room, after dark, in the altogether, in front of all those windows. So I managed to close enough drapes to shield me somewhat.

They lent us their second car, a Honda Prelude, and we drove to the town of Kinloch on Lake Taupo. The Honda had plenty of legroom, but Doug's head hit the roof any time we went over a bump. Fortunately, the car had a sunroof, so he popped it a bit and had lots of room. It was a good thing he was comfortable as we couldn't believe how busy the road was. There wasn't much in our direction, which was good, but bumper to bumper going back to the city. The trip to Kinloch was through rolling country with some low hills, mostly farmland and ranches. Doug said it reminded him of Nova Scotia. The big difference was that the hills there were mostly cinder cones from old volcanoes. This part of New Zealand was full of hot springs and boiling mud pools, the most famous being Rotorua. We had been here several years ago on our bus trip through New Zealand. We had a little trouble finding the house as the address we had was Island Drive. After driving around where we thought we should be, we realized we were missing a letter in our instructions and we were actually looking for Lisland Drive. Once we found it, we were very pleased with the house. It was beautiful but a little larger than we were used to. It was a 4-bedroom, 3-bathroom house, long and low and all on one level.

On our first trip into the town of Taupo we found out why there was so much traffic on the road the day before. There were crews out removing barriers and taking down signs and banners welcoming the athletes to the Ironman Triathlon. We were glad we hadn't come two days earlier while the race was on.

We spent the day as we usually do on our first day in a new location; shopping for groceries, looking for a coffee shop and getting a feel for the place. This time we had something new, we had to find an internet café. This was the first house we'd stayed at on this trip with no internet. Both the Perth and Melbourne houses had broadband we could connect to. This one, out in the country and being a vacation home, didn't even have a phone, so we couldn't even do dial-up. Any internet had to be done at a café.

We were also having a little trouble with the Kiwi dialect. We'd often joked about Aussies speaking English...sort of, but New Zealanders put a different spin on the language as well. For instance, what we call a shopping cart or buggy, Aussies call a trolley and NZers call a trundler. New Zealanders also have a funny way of pronouncing the letters FI; it sounds like FU. Fifty dollars sounds like fufty dollars, and fish sounds like fush. Aussies pronounce the A like an I, as in whale sounds like while, and mate sounds like mite. You have to listen hard and mentally translate what's been said. New Zealand also makes use of the Maori language in place names and street names. We were staying in Kinloch, a Scottish name, but to get to the town of Taupo we drove along Whangamata Rd, turned right on Poihipi Rd, turned right again on Ohuhiri. I'm sure if some of the local people had heard my pronunciations as I told Doug what road to turn on, they would have laughed their heads off.

Once we got settled, we went to a tourist bureau in town to see what sightseeing options there are in this area. One thing we thought we'd like to do is a jetboat ride on the river, as we had done this before in NZ and enjoyed it. However, the information person mentioned that this particular one got a bit rough as it goes right up to the waterfall and he advised us to bring a change of clothes as we were almost certain to get wet. As it was now fall in NZ and some days were chilly, we decided that spending a couple of hours out on the river in wet clothes was not a good idea. One woman in the tourist bureau heard our accents and said she was going to our part of the world that summer and asked if we could answer some questions. It turned out that she was going to Las Vegas, which isn't exactly our part of the world, but it's still a city we know well, so we were able to give her some advice on places to stay and things to do. One piece of information that surprised her was that the temperature in Las Vegas could easily be over 100F in the summer, so she'd better be prepared for that. In fact, we were in Vegas one year in June and the temp hit 113 at midday.

One day when we were out shopping in Taupo we stopped for lunch at a small bakery café. As it was crowded, we had to share a table. The single lady at our table was a very interesting person from Essex, England. She was 80 years old and had been travelling for about three months in China, Bangkok and Japan the first month, then Australia and now New Zealand. She was travelling by herself and she used one of my favourite traveling tricks. She said she started out with a suitcase full of old clothes, and as she shopped for new things or gifts for her grandkids, she discarded her old things to make room. Her last discard before she heads for home will be all her part containers of toiletries like shampoo, skin cream and toothpaste. I guess I'm not the only one who does that.

The part of New Zealand we were staying was a geo-thermal area, full of hot springs and hot mud pits. One day we visited an area that was totally different from anything we'd experienced before. It was called Craters of the Moon. This was a sunken area, surrounded by hills, that looks like a crater itself. It was probably a couple of kilometers across and dotted with small craters or cracks with hot steam pouring out of them. In the parking lot we were wearing jackets as there was a chilly wind, but as we walked along the pathways and boardwalks between the craters it was so warm from the steam that we soon took off the jackets. We were told to stay on the paths as the ground was unstable and some people who ignored this and wandered off occasionally broke through the thin crust into the hot stuff below and ended up with burned feet. In fact, we saw one footprint where someone had recently done just that. It took us about an hour to walk around the perimeter of the crater, looking into some of the steam holes. At one point we took a side trip to a mud pool and that was the most dramatic. The bottom of this pool was covered with a grey ash-colored mud and it was actually boiling. Bubbles rose to the surface and broke in a puff of steam. It was also making a bubbling and hissing noise. I put my camera on video and shot about a one minute of the boiling mud. We also had the option of climbing a hill for an overview of the crater, but as it was listed as a steep climb up and 153 steps down, we decided not to do it.

The complex also included a glassblowers' studio and gallery. It was called Lava Glass and some of the stuff was beautiful. I would have loved to own a piece, but at several hundred dollars for some of the vases and into the thousands for some of the larger pieces, it was way outside my budget.

On another day of sightseeing, we had a big lesson in history and geography and marvelled at the possible interconnection between their country and ours. We went first to a place called Wairakei Terraces. These were hot springs tumbling over a waterfall that had developed into terraces covered in the silica that the hot springs produce. 150 years ago these terraces were fantastic formations, but were destroyed in 1886 in a huge eruption. In recent years, the local Maoris had diverted the hotsprings into a river and created artificial terraces and waterfalls. The natural silica has covered the rocks and the terraces are now getting back to looking much like they did before the eruption.

The walk through the gardens and along the river took about an hour and we saw replicas of Maori villages and sacred places. All the wooden carvings were done locally.

We had a long talk with a Maori carver about the tikis and totems around the place. We commented that the totem poles were much like the Haida Indian totems that we see back home, and he said that a few years ago they had an exchange of carvers at Rotorua. A carver from Canada came and carved a totem pole with an eagle on top and a Maori carver went to Canada and carved one of his tribal totems. He also told us the story of how the Maoris came to New Zealand, and it is remarkably like the story the Hawaiians tell of how they came to Hawaii. Then we had a discussion of the likenesses between the Maori, Hawaiian and Haida cultures and speculated on the possibility that, in the distant past, they may have had a common ancestry. A delightful and interesting conversation that we're really glad we had.

There was also a hot pool there called the Healing Pool, and the receptionist told us we were welcome to dip our feet or hands in the pool if they were in need of help, and that it was very good for arthritis. We both took off our shoes and put our feet in the pool. I don't know if it was the power of suggestion or what, but we both had sore feet after walking around the gardens for over an hour, and after soaking them in the hot sulphur pool, our feet felt great on the walk back.

The geography lesson came in the next place we visited, the Volcanic Activity Centre. It explained how New Zealand is the most volcano and earthquake prone zone in the world. Two major tectonic plates meet in NZ, and the rift travels the whole length of the country. Most major events happen on the North Island, but the South Island occasionally gets them as well. One of their attractions is a room which simulates the 6.5 earthquake that hit near this area a few years ago. We were seated on benches around the room and it literally knocked us off them. We had to hold on tight to keep from landing on the floor. We also saw a movie documenting the 1996 volcanic eruption in a mountain just south of Lake Taupo. The mountain is a ski resort and the eruption happened in June when the ski season was in full swing. It showed people at the resort complaining because the lifts were closed and they couldn't ski or snowboard. Then it showed a huge car-sized boulder that shot out of the crater and rolled down the mountain taking out one of the lift chairs. That put an end to the complaining and the owners eventually closed the resort for the season and laid off the staff, as the eruption continued into July. It also showed local scenic helicopters taking photographers up close to the crater. One pilot who was interviewed said he often flew clients into the crater and landed beside the lake at the bottom of the crater. Now the crater was spewing ash and rocks and smoke and he was being careful of how close he flew as you never knew what was coming out next. We also saw a documentary called Land in Motion that pinpointed volcanic mountains all over the country that had either erupted in recent memory or were classified as likely to in the near future. Part of it was also on earthquakes and the damage they do to people and property. It was a very interesting and informative day and we were so glad we got to experience it. We consider all travel to be a learning experience, but our visit to New Zealand really was an education.

Lake Taupo, which we were living on the shores of, is actually a extinct volcanic crater that has become filled with water. It is ringed with high cliffs and cinder cones. We could see a distinctive cinder cone out our dining room window, probably about three kilometers away. Lake Rotorua, about 100 km away is also a volcanic crater. As both lakes are ringed with hot springs and boiling mud pools, the earth's crust is very thin there. The very thing that makes it such a popular tourist resort could someday make it a very dangerous place to live.

After a couple of days of intense walking it was time for a little down time, so we opted for Shawn's Prawn Park for lunch. There is a huge geo-thermal plant near Taupo and a few years ago someone discovered that prawns thrived in the warm water near the outflow of the plant into the river. So they set up a prawn farm to breed and grow prawns for sale. It eventually evolved in a sort of theme park with people taking tours in the farm and being allowed to fish for their own prawns to take home. We passed on the prawn fishing as they didn't look like they were catching anything. All we really wanted was a prawn lunch that someone else cooked. We had lunch on the patio overlooking the river where the jetboats go, and it was interesting to watch them go by. For lunch we had a prawn and salad platter for two. The prawns were HUGE, nothing shrimpy about them. The only problem was the mess. They came complete with heads with whiskers, as well as claws, and we had to snap the heads off and peel them before eating. Lunch took a bit longer than we'd planned.

One thing about living in someone else's house is that you're not used to the ambient noises. One night we had a bit of a scare. First of all, since these were mainly holiday homes not all of them were occupied. We had no close neighbours; the houses on either side were empty as was the house across the street. Shortly after 11 pm we were sitting reading and heard a noise outside. Then there was a sort of bang on the roof, and more noises outside. We turned on all the outside lights but there was nothing there. We even went outside in the backyard, but still nothing. We heard a few small noises but couldn't pinpoint where they were coming from. Finally, when we didn't hear anything for a while we went to bed. Next morning, we went out and walked all around the house and had a good look in the light. There was a fence on one side of the house, near the garage roof overhang, and just above it, on the roof, were muddy footprints, or paw prints. We had no idea what kind of critters live around there, but one of them was on our roof that night, possibly a raccoon. Once we knew about it, we could laugh about it, but it wasn't a laughing matter the previous night.

One day when we got back after being to the market there was a helicopter parked on the lawn of the house across the street. Not just landed there but parked for a while with a sunshield tied across the windshield. The house across the street was now occupied. We knew we were in an upscale neighborhood, but neighbours who come up for the weekend by helicopter were a little more upscale than we're used to.

After a couple of misty days, we finally got a nice sunny day so we could take our boat trip on the lake. We opted for the brunch cruise, so we can now say that we had brunch in the center of the crater of an extinct volcano. For lunch we were parked next to a 50-foot spire of hardened lava, surrounded by 1000-foot cliffs on three sides. The boat captain told us the spire was the plug in the center of the crater. It was not really a comfortable feeling. A few kilometers across the lake a cone-shaped island could be seen sticking out of the water and we were told that there is still volcanic activity at its base underwater. And just behind that island was the ski mountain that exploded in 1996, the one we saw the movie of in the Volcanic Activity Center. I don't imagine we were the only ones wondering what would happen to us if that lava plug let go.

During the trip we saw some Maori carvings in the rocks on the edge of the lake. We also got a history of the area. The big eruption that caused the current shape of Lake Taupo happened 1800 years ago in the year 184 AD. There was no one living there at that time, but they were able to pinpoint the date because of records kept by the Chinese and also in Rome, which mentioned "three days of night, when smoke and ash blocked out the sun."

We couldn't leave New Zealand without trying one of their outdoor hot springs. The one we chose to visit had all natural pools surrounded with rocks and plants. We soaked in the hot springs for over an hour at three different pools, warm, hot and hottest. We were told that the natural spring water there is so hot that they have to mix it with cold for the pools. One stream coming out of the side of a hill was almost boiling. Neither of us could stay in the third, or hottest, pool for more than a few minutes. After soaking in the pools, we visited the attached spa where they gave us warm fleecy robes to wear. Doug had a massage and I had a manicure and pedicure. It was nice to be pampered as we'd done some tough walking and hiking on this trip.

However, the toughest walk was to come the next day after the spa when we walked 800 steps, 400 up and 400 down. If I had known what I was in for, I never would have gone. We decided to have a last New Zealand Maori experience, as we only had a couple of days left. Someone, obviously younger and more agile than us, recommended a thermal area called Orakei Korako. We were told it is one of the best and the brochures were very promising. But nothing mentioned the steps. When we arrived at the location in a hidden valley about 25 kms from Taupo, we could see the silica fields across a lake. We were taken across the lake in a boat and given a map. The map showed a circle tour of several locations of silica terraces, hot springs and geysers and boiling mud pits, as well as a cave with water and a small beach. We climbed a few stairs to a small landing where we could see the silica fields and their color. They were fantastic, virtually every color in the spectrum. Then some more steps to the top of a small terrace of more pools. When more steps led to the cave, I knew I was in trouble. Here we were about a third of the way around. The dilemma - do we go back, not having seen the best parts? Or do we go on, hoping it would level out? Then we found that the cave was at the bottom of about 50 steps. It was a large cave that contained a lake and a beach and there were people swimming. What we could see from the top was beautiful, but adding another 100 steps to what we knew would be tough climb, was not an option. People coming up the stairs were walking very slowly, obviously tired as the steps went straight down, with no landings.

We hadn't seen the mud pools yet, but after a few more minutes of climbing we realized we were at the very top. On the way up, we both had to sit down and rest a few times, mostly by sitting on the stairs as there were very few benches. As we started back down I decided to count the steps and got to 404 before we got back down to the dock to catch the boat back across the lake. The trip back down was not good; my knees were in bad shape by the time we finished. Doug, who is used to walking more than me, also had sore knees.

Our last day there was spent as it usually is, cleaning, laundry and packing. The next day we left Lake Taupo and drove back to Hamilton for an overnight flight home.

Our flight back home was a little different, although we'd known what to expect for a while and were prepared for it. We were flying first class on points, but when we booked it several months previously, we found out that Air Canada only allocated one first class seat per flight on points. Their reasoning was that mainly single business passengers travelled in first class on points. We argued that discriminated against couples travelling together, but it was policy and no breaking it. Singapore Airlines had no problem with us flying together and neither did Air New Zealand that we flew from Melbourne to Auckland. But the flight back on the day we wanted was on Air Canada, not on either of those. I was flying back on Air Canada to Vancouver on a direct flight that night, while Doug had to fly to Sydney on AC, stay overnight there and then fly Sydney to Vancouver the next day. So, we flew this last leg of the journey separately and I got home a day earlier than Doug.

This had been our longest and most complicated trip. We were away three months, did three separate exchanges, visited three different countries, flew on three different airlines, had three different train journeys. Thoroughly satisfied, on the final flight, I lay down on the newly configured single, fully-reclining seat, pulled the duvet up, and slept the whole way home.

Chapter 8

REVISITING FAMILIAR PLACES AND
CHANGING PLANS AS WE GO

AFTER OUR BUSY AND demanding three country trips in 2008, the next winter was shaping up to be quite different. My left knee had bothered me for several years and was getting worse, so it was time to do something about it. I went through a battery of tests and X-rays and was eventually informed that I needed a knee replacement. I was placed on the waitlist for surgery, but then found out that the wait time was anywhere from six to twelve months. By now, it was December and a long cold winter stretched ahead of us with no plans.

Then one day sitting at the computer I got a pop-up ad from a hotel in Honolulu advertising two weeks in a studio apartment for a price too good to refuse. We had heard that, as a result of a recession in Japan, Hawaiian tourism was in a slump. It looked like Hawaii really needed us, and right then we really needed Hawaii. We booked it for the last two weeks in January. Then realizing that February weather at home was really no better than January, we did an online search and found another condo in the Ilikai Hotel right across the street that we booked for a second two weeks. So we had a month in Honolulu booked for mid-January to mid-February. Through our credit card we had a $99 return companion flight from Kelowna to Honolulu, so we even got that at a discount.

Then about a week after we made those arrangements, we got a e-mail from a couple in Maroochydore, Queensland, asking if we would like an exchange for two months, February and March. They were both teachers and were on their sabbatical year, and wanted to spend the first two months of it skiing at Big White. We were about to turn down the offer as we already had plans for the worst part of winter, when Doug reminded me of a discussion we had shortly after we returned from our last trip. He said then that he thought we were done with Australia but if we ever got an offer from Maroochydore he might reconsider as the Sunshine Coast and Maroochydore in particular was his favourite part of the country.

With this in mind, we considered the implications, looked up flights and came up with a plan. We e-mailed the couple, I'll call them Jim and Kelly, accepted their exchange offer and told them we would be in Hawaii for a month, starting January 15, so they could come two weeks early if they wished. But that we wouldn't arrive at their place until mid-February as we'd already made plans to stay in Honolulu until then. They decided they would come early, so that's what we agreed on. That meant that we would not go home from Hawaii but fly directly to Brisbane, Australia, from there.

I should add here that to enter Australia from another country you need a visa. If you are travelling as a tourist or on a short business trip, this can be purchased electronically online. If you input your passport number, country of origin and date of entering Australia during the purchase process, it will be electronically linked to your passport so when you enter the country and your passport is scanned the visa purchase will be noted and your passport stamped. This only applies to short visits. If you plan to work or study in Australia the visa process is more detailed and can't be done online.

We looked up flights on one of those websites that compares several airlines and found that Hawaiian Airlines was the cheapest. We had flown Hawaiian between the islands before but never on a long international flight, but decided to go for it. I can say right now that it was an excellent decision as we loved flying Hawaiian. The flight attendants were dressed in Hawaiian dresses, the drink of choice was a Mai Tai and the whole flight was a festive experience. We've since flown with them twice more and would do it again.

We enjoyed our month in Honolulu. There were several couples from Kelowna that we knew, who were in Honolulu at that time. They were staying at various hotels, and got together every day at 4 pm for Happy Hour. We happily joined them and took our turn hosting. About once a week all of us went out to dinner together, and our third week there I arranged for the whole group to go on a circle island tour. The tour included a stop at one of the North Shore's famous shrimp trucks for lunch. We have subsequently returned to Honolulu several times, each time reconnecting with the same group and enjoying Happy Hours.

The apartment we rented on that trip was in the Ilikai complex. There is absolutely nothing like sitting on a balcony overlooking the ocean, watching the sun go down while sipping Mai Tais.

When we were first planning this trip, we were afraid that packing a suitcase for two trips might be a bit difficult, but as we got into it we realized that both Hawaii and Australia are warm weather places, so the same clothes would do for both. We already had power adapters for our electronics from our previous trips, so we were okay there.

By the way, Australian electrical power is 220, double our 110, and their plugs are three-pronged with the prongs angled differently from ours. So, you not only need an adapter for the plug to fit, but a power-reducing adapter if you don't want to fry your phone.

After a month in Hawaii we were ready for our new adventure in Australia, although this time it would be in a place we had visited twice before and knew well.

Our overnight flight to Brisbane on Hawaiian Air was uneventful and we caught the short commuter flight on Jetblue to the Maroochydore airport. From there we took a taxi to where we would stay for the next six weeks. It was a beautiful apartment with a great view out over the ocean, terraces on three sides with loads of plants and outdoor furniture, that we would greatly enjoy over the next six weeks.

Not far from where we were staying was a Surf Club. We could see the ocean and the Surf Club from our terrace. Our second day there we checked it out and purchased a non-resident membership for our stay. Their big thing was their restaurant, and they had a list of specialty nights; Monday was pasta night, Tuesday was burger night, Wednesday was roast night, etc. Our favorite was seafood night, which was usually on Saturday. They also had a light lunch buffet of salads and sandwiches, presumably for business people as it was served Monday to Friday. We went several times and enjoyed our lunches outside on the deck overlooking the beach and the ocean. Just offshore was a peculiar shaped island. We never did find out what it was called, but as it looked very much like a beached whale, we referred to it as the Whale Island.

About our third day there we got a call from our hosts' friend, Dave, a fellow teacher whom they worked with. He called to see how we were doing, and invited us to a barbecue that weekend. He said they were a group of five couples, only two of which were teachers, who got together once a week. He said everyone contributed to the evening and we could bring a vegetable dish if we wished. I decided to make my favourite vegetable casserole of broccoli, cauliflower and carrots, baked in a mushroom cream sauce and topped with shredded cheese. We were surprised when we arrived to find we'd brought the only hot dish except for the meat cooked on the Barbie. In Australia, being a hot country, salads and chilled dishes are more popular than hot. We made note of that and didn't make that mistake again on subsequent get-togethers. The weekend barbeques weren't always at someone's house; one week we met at the beach and cooked on one of the communal barbecue grills that are found on most public beaches.

At one of these get-togethers, I asked for some advice on restaurants. I mentioned that Doug had a birthday coming up and wondered where would be a good place to go for dinner. They all looked at me with shocked expressions and one of them said: "You can't celebrate a birthday alone. It just isn't done. We're all coming along as well." Then there was a lively discussion as to where we would go and which place could handle all of us with ease. Doug and I had no part in this discussion; we just sat there and listened. When a calendar appeared and it was discovered that his birthday was on a Saturday, the discussion was over. The seafood buffet at the Surf Club won out. One of the men offered to make the reservation with the Surf Club and ask for a special table to be set up for us. He would send everyone an e-mail with the confirmation and time.

That birthday celebration was memorable. Besides the delicious food, there were several bottles of wine on the table and a pile of gifts. Doug had fun opening the gifts. They were all local fun things like a calendar with photos of local beaches with girls in bikinis, a ball cap with a Queensland beer logo, a jar of Vegemite (that awful smelling stuff that Aussie kids eat like we do peanut butter), and a book on how to 'speak Aussie'. When they sang Happy Birthday, everyone in the restaurant joined in. At the end of the evening, we all lined up on a stairwell and got someone to take our photo with my camera. It was a birthday celebration we will never forget, made even more special by the fact that we were accepted, not as strangers in their land, but as friends who had come to visit. My gift for him was a polo shirt with the Surf Club's logo. It's still hanging in his closet and he still wears it sometimes. Every time he does wear

135

it one of us will mention that trip and the wonderful people we met there.

One day we had another visit with our friends Doug and Terry from Brisbane. Maroochydore is about an hour's drive north of Brisbane. They drove up to see us and stayed for the weekend. It was interesting to see little Daniel. The last time we saw him he was just a baby and this time he was running nonstop all over the place.

As we'd been to this area before there wasn't much new to see, so we revisited some places we'd enjoyed before. We went to the Eumundi Market one day. Another day we revisited the Big Pineapple.

One place that was a little sad to visit was the Australian Zoo. The owner, Steve Irwin, had died since we'd been last and the place was being run by his family. There was a memorial to Steve in the park and we walked through it, reading stories of his life. A lot of it we knew, as we never missed an episode of his show when it was on TV. The previous time we'd been there the staff were playing with some small lion cubs. This time the lions were fully grown but the staff were still playing with them as if they were cubs. It was amazing how tame the lions were, but I suppose the zoo was the only life they had ever known.

When it came time to go back home, we flew back to Honolulu on Hawaiian Air and stayed there for a few days before returning home. Neither of us likes the long 16-hour flight from Australia to Vancouver, so we prefer to break it up into two flights and cut the jet lag a bit.

Chapter 9

THE BEST LAID PLANS DON'T ALWAYS WORK OUT

THE SUMMER AFTER OUR exchange to Maroochydore was our 50th wedding anniversary and we had some ambitious plans to celebrate the occasion. We had done several ocean cruises, but thought we would like to try a river cruise in Europe that year. We booked a cruise from Budapest to Nuremburg the last week in September. As Doug also wanted to visit the town of Dierdorf, the ancestral home of the Kaulbachs, we looked for an exchange in Germany, somewhere near Frankfurt. We found one in the Mosel area, a couple named Gunter and Brenna. The exchange was arranged for three weeks, starting the last week in August. We corresponded with them while we were in Australia and after we returned. Gunter even looked up the phone book in Dierdorf and told us there were 10 Kaulbachs still listed, so we were very excited about visiting there.

Our anniversary was August 1 and we had a party planned at our clubhouse with over 100 people invited, including relatives from all across the country, and also Doug's cousins from Manchester, England. Following the anniversary party, we had booked a house at Silver Star resort for several days for just ourselves, our kids, their spouses and our grandkids. Then, when everyone else had left, the British cousins were to stay with us for another week. We had everything planned and organized. Then disaster struck.

Two weeks before our anniversary I fell and broke my leg. It was a bad fracture that involved surgery, two screws inserted to hold it together and a three-day hospital stay. With all plans made, the venue booked and family coming from all across the country, there was no way we could cancel the party. I went to my 50th anniversary party in a wheelchair.

Luckily family pitched in to help. One brother and his wife offered to decorate the hall. I had already purchased the decorations so we had those available. My sister and two sisters-in-law volunteered to run the kitchen, heating the hors d'oeuvres and setting out the desserts. I sat there in splendor in the dress I had purchased for the occasion, my broken leg sticking out in front with bare toes showing. Actually, except for the initial shock at my appearance, no one noticed me. The stars of the show were our two granddaughters, Kacey, aged 2 ½ and Kailyn, aged 6 weeks. Kacey obviously thought the party was for her as she ran around greeting everyone, socializing with anyone who would talk to her, stopping every few minutes to snitch another cookie from the buffet, climbing into her Daddy's arms and grabbing the mic while he was trying to toast the occasion and finally falling asleep on the couch. Kailyn, who slept the whole time snuggled into a sling across her mother's chest, was a big hit. Everyone had to see her, touch her hair and exclaim what a good baby she was.

The next day we all went to the house up at Silver Star. Silver Star is a ski resort, but they also have activities there in the summer, and the summer rent is much lower. At first, we thought we might have to cancel as we knew the house was two floors and there were about 12 steps up to the first floor from the street. But when we contacted the owner and explained the situation, he said that, as the house was on a slope, the back of the house actually had only two steps up to a porch where they usually stored skis, and that porch opened into the kitchen. He said he and a friend would go up there before we arrived and build a ramp for the wheelchair at the back. He also told us that a room off the living room on the lower level that they used for an office had a couch that opened into a double bed, and that the lower level also had a bathroom between the office and the kitchen. I could sleep there instead of trying to go upstairs to the bedrooms.

They were so accommodating and it looked like it would work, so we went. And everything worked just fine.

Shortly after the accident we had contacted the German couple and explained that we would not be able to go to their place right now, but they could still come if they wished and stay in our guest bedroom. We would lend them my car, as I was certainly not driving at this point, and they could do all the sightseeing they would have done had we not been here. They opted to do that and we enjoyed hosting them. They were a delightful couple, and as I was on crutches and a bit more mobile by the time they arrived, we were able to go with them to some of the places. As this was the summer before the Vancouver Winter Olympics, they wanted to see the ski venue at Whistler, so we gave them a map with the route to Whistler marked and they went off in my car by themselves. They came back for a few days, then took the car again for a three-day circle trip through the Rockies. They enjoyed their stay here and we enjoyed having them. They still owe us a stay at their place, but we haven't taken them up on it.

The other thing we had to do was cancel our flights to Germany and the river cruise. We usually buy cancellation insurance for our trips and this was one time we were certainly glad we did. We would have been out thousands of dollars if we hadn't

After doing this a few times you learn to be flexible. In our eight years exchanging with Australians, we had two couples who let us stay in their house but never came to ours. And we've had two, including this one, that went the other way, with them staying in our house, but we never went to theirs.

The other thing that got changed was my surgery appointment to have a knee replacement. It was originally scheduled for the summer but I had it deferred until October when our anniversary festivities, the Germany exchange and river cruise would be over. When I broke my leg, the orthopedic surgeon who fixed it was the same surgeon who was scheduled to do the knee replacement. The fracture, which was in the other leg, was quite near the knee and when he saw me in hospital, his first comment was "Too bad you didn't break the other knee, then I could have done two jobs in one." His other comment, when I was discharged from hospital, was that the replacement surgery would have to be put off for six months. He said that major surgery was too hard on the system to have two so close together, and I also needed to have at least one good leg to stand on.

The knee replacement surgery was rescheduled for the following February so we made no plans for an exchange that winter. Instead, we went to Toronto to visit our son and family for Christmas and from there flew to Florida and went on a Caribbean cruise.

The surgery went well and I was still on crutches when we started planning our next exchange.

Chapter 10

A DIFFERENT EXCHANGE, CLOSER TO HOME

IN THE SPRING OF 2010 we got a exchange offer from a couple in Calgary, Alberta. They were looking at retiring within a year and Kelowna was the place they were interested in. They saw on our profile on the Homelink website that we lived in a detached house in a retirement community with a clubhouse and activities, and that was the lifestyle they thought they would like. They had never lived in our style community before and wanted to actually live here and participate in the community activities to see if they liked it. So they asked for a one month exchange, offering us their condo near downtown Calgary with a view of the river and the city. They also told us they were contacting another couple with similar living accommodations.

The other couple they contacted happened to be friends of ours, Don and Jean, who live five doors from us on the same street, and whom we introduced to home exchanging. We got together and discussed it, and as neither of us wanted to exchange in the summer for a month, we agreed to make the Calgary couple an offer. We would split the exchange, if we could go for the Calgary Stampede. None of us had ever been to the Stampede and this seemed like a good chance to do it.

So we contacted the Calgary couple, Bob and Jenna. They had never heard of splitting an exchange, and neither had we, but we discussed it and came to an agreement. We would go to Calgary for the week before the Stampede and the first week of the two-week event, and Don and Jean would go for the second week of the Stampede and stay one week after. Bob and Jenna would stay in our house for two weeks and then move to Don and Jean's house.

The exchanges went well and everyone enjoyed the exchange experience. However, Bob and Jenna decided not to live in a senior's community as the houses were too small for their purpose. Bob was an artist and required a large room for a studio and Jenna was still doing some consulting work and needed an office. The exchange was a success for them as it helped them to decide what they didn't want.

We enjoyed our two weeks in Calgary and did a lot more than just going to the Stampede. We also did our key exchange in a different way. We had planned to visit friends in Edmonton for a few days before the exchange, so said we would stop by and pick up the keys on the way through Calgary. As we planned to stop overnight in Canmore, only about an hour's drive from Calgary, they invited us for breakfast to exchange keys. Bob, in addition to being an artist is also a chef, so we had a most delicious breakfast and tour of their condo.

The Calgary condo, on the 8th floor, had perhaps the best view in Calgary. It looked out over a park where there were team sports going on every day. Then just past the park was the train station to downtown, and beyond that the river. On the other side of the river was the Stampede Grounds. We could see the stadium where the rodeo took place, and also the Saddledome stadium where the Calgary Flames hockey team played. Off to the right we could see the tall buildings of downtown Calgary. Their balcony was a great place to just sit and watch things happening.

Once we'd settled in, we took the train downtown to do a bit of exploring. One place we went was the Calgary Tower, which is so tall we could see as far as the foothills of the Rockies. One part of the tower deck had a glass floor where you could stand and watch the traffic way below by looking between your feet. Scary!!!

We had always heard that the Calgary Zoo was a good one so we decided to do that one day before the stampede opened. The animals were much like any other zoo we'd seen, but we were blown away by the spectacular Dinosaur Exhibit. This was a separate place where we walked through trees and towering rocks and every time we turned a corner there was a different life-size dinosaur. Some of them were huge and most were animated. One tall one opened its mouth and roared as you got near. Another one's tail whipped around and you had to stay out of its way. We were glad we didn't live when those things roamed the earth.

As Stampede opening day got closer, the excitement downtown ramped up. People were walking the streets in western gear and the first of the pancake breakfasts opened up. Traditionally, downtown businesses put up barbecues outside on the sidewalks as well as huge griddles for cooking pancakes. The barbecues were for sausages or bacon or whatever they decided would make a good "go with" for the pancakes. Most of the food was free, although some asked for donations for a specific charity.

For people not acquainted with the Calgary Stampede, it's an annual event which bills itself as "The Greatest Outdoor Show on Earth." It attracts over one million visitors every year and features one of the world's largest rodeos, as well as a huge parade, a midway, stage shows, concerts, agricultural competitions and, the most popular attraction, the chuckwagon races.

We went to the parade and it was great fun. We went early with our folding chairs and staked out a spot on the sidewalk. There was no shade, so the one hour wait and the 2 ½ hour long parade required a lot of sunscreen and water. There were a lot of marching bands and walking groups but we enjoyed the ones with the character balloons. The two best floats were probably WestJet and Air Canada. They both had large airplane-shaped balloons tethered above their floats. The float we cheered the loudest for was Kelowna's Ogopogo.

We were told that the first day of the Stampede was always the busiest, so we waited and went on the second day. It still seemed very busy and crowded to us, but it is known world-wide, so that was to be expected. We were surprised to find that there was an ice show on so we went to that. There were several skaters interspersed with acrobatics, so we stayed in that building for quite a while. We'd seen two of the skaters before and one of them, Elvis Stojko, not only skated solo but did a pairs routine with his new wife, a figure skater from Mexico. Elvis Stojko is one of Canada's best figure skaters, having won World and Olympic figure skating medals as well as winning the Canadian championship seven times. We went back later in the day, just to see Elvis skate again.

We spent the rest of the day looking at exhibits and eating at booths and then took the skyway cable chairs back across the fair-grounds. A couple of days later we went back and this time sat in the stands and watched several rodeo events, including a chuckwagon race. The chuckwagon races were quite exciting at the start as each of the competitors battled for position. But not long into the race they were strung out in a line and from then on, the positions usually didn't vary, so the endings were predictable unless one of them rolled over on a curve. The two times that happened, the pileups were spectacular. Perhaps that was what people went to see, not the actual races. The Stampede was something we're glad we got to see, but not something we would be interested in doing again.

We were lucky that the weather was so good when we were in Calgary. We had lovely sunny weather every day. A week later when Don and Jean were there, they had a very heavy rainstorm that turned into hail. Hail is sometimes a precursor to a tornado on the prairies, but luckily this time it didn't happen. There was a lot of damage to cars from the hail but not to theirs as it was parked in the condo's underground garage.

All three couples enjoyed this unusual split exchange, and several months later when Bob and Jenna moved to Kelowna, they invited us to dinner at their house. As we were all experienced exchangers, we had a lively evening discussing our experiences.

Chapter 11

THREE EXCHANGES IN OUR HOME PROVINCE OF BRITISH COLUMBIA

ALTHOUGH OUR EXCHANGES TO the other side of the world are the ones we usually talk about, we did do three low-key exchanges to Vancouver Island. Each of them was in the summer, lasted only one week and we all drove our own vehicles. Over the years, talking to other exchangers and reading online blogs, we've come to the conclusion that there are essentially two types of home exchangers. There are adventurers, like us, who travel to countries all over the world, and those who prefer short trips close by where they can drive their own car. Sometimes a couple will choose a short exchange as their first one, just to see if they like it. As for us, Vancouver Island is a place where we love to visit, where we have friends, and where we've never turned down an exchange offer.

The first Island exchange was to Victoria and it was early in our exchanging days, being only our second exchange. R and D wanted to come to Kelowna for a week to attend a conference on the weekend and then to spend some time golfing. They advertised their house as being a Victoria heritage house that had been renovated. In reality they'd built a whole new house on the back of a small old house. The front of the house with dormer window, front porch and steps leading to the front door was all that was left of the original house. From the street the look of the heritage house was unchanged, but once inside the front door and past the porch with its seat and pegs for hanging coats, the house was a beautiful two storey modern home.

Early in our exchange of e-mails they mentioned allergies and the fact they were attracted to our listing because of the "no pets and no smoking" conditions. We confirmed that we were a pet-free and smoke-free house and that we also had some allergies, one of which was to perfumes and fragrances. We mentioned that all our clothes, towels and bedding were laundered in scent-free detergents and fabric softeners. Further along in our correspondence they brought up the subject of food allergies, saying that one of them was allergic to peppers, nuts and nut products and sesame seeds. When we eventually did this exchange, I made sure we had none of the mentioned products in the fridge or any of the cupboards. I almost messed up in their kitchen one day while making sandwiches for lunch. I realized I was using buns with sesame seeds on them, I immediately transferred everything to paper towels and scrubbed the knife and cutting board in hot soapy water.

We enjoyed that exchange. They had a nice comfy king bed and a sunny back patio to sit on and read. While there we visited our friends, Gerry and Maureen, who live in Sooke and invited them to dinner at "our" house. We also did a lot of sightseeing including the fabulous Butchart Gardens.

Our second exchange to Vancouver Island was in the town of Duncan, on the eastern shore of the Island. We arrived there on a rainy day with heavy cloud cover and a forecast for more of the same. We knew that Island weather was often wet, so resigned ourselves to a gloomy week. However, we woke the next morning to a marvelous surprise. Not only was the sun shining, but when we stepped out on the deck at the back of the house, there in the distance was the snow-capped peak of Mount Baker. We'd seen Mount Baker up close and from all angles, so recognized it immediately, but had no idea it could be seen from such a distance. We were probably 80 miles from its base. The whole time we were there the first thing I did each morning was check to see if Mount Baker was still there. Only one morning was it lost in the fog. The rest of the time we enjoyed the view, sometimes perfectly clear, other times with a puffy cloud caught on the summit.

On this trip we connected with another retired Royal Banker, named George, and his wife, who live in the next town. We'd been corresponding by e-mail for several years but had never met.

We also re-connected with our friends, Gerry and Maureen in Sooke, getting there by taking the road less travelled. We drove to Sooke the short, but bumpy, way over the mountain from Duncan to Renfrew, then along the coast road to Sooke. There is a ridge of mountain that runs the length of the Island from north to south and this is the only road that crosses it in the middle. It was a rough road at that time and we occasionally had to put our vehicle in 4-wheel-drive, but we made it. That trip qualifies as an adventure.

When we arrived in Sooke, instead of going to our friends' house we went to a music festival near the beach. This is a yearly festival and they were both working it as volunteers. We stayed with them that night and drove back home the next day.

A short explanation as to who Gerry and Maureen are: officially they are our daughter's in-laws. However, from the first time we met we hit it off and have become friends. After a couple of visits with the kids along, we now visit back and forth without them. We have a lot in common, we love wine, board games, books and travelling. We affectionately refer to each other as the out-laws.

Our third Vancouver Island exchange was actually our last real exchange. This was another heritage house right in the downtown area of Victoria. This one was different from the other in that the outside of the house was still original. It was a big two storey house with an attic. It had an open porch that ran the full width of the front of the house and was full of plants and wicker furniture. The driveway and parking area were behind a high wooden fence, so from the street it looked much as it would have looked in the early 1900s. Inside was a totally different story. The ground floor had been gutted and modernized. It had wooden floors, ceramic tile, and a modern kitchen that wouldn't have looked out of place in a magazine. This was modern living with a vintage façade.

The upstairs was a mix of the two. The bathrooms were small, but sported up to the minute facilities. The beds were comfortable and queen-sized. Closets were non-existent so a couple of the smaller rooms had been turned into closets with hanging rods and lots of shelving. The only problem with the upstairs was that the doorways were still the original. The openings were all about six feet, which gave my 6'3" husband a problem; especially when he had to go to the bathroom in the middle of the night and forgot to duck.

We were there for a week and for the last two days our daughter, Kristal, who lived in Vancouver, came to visit. She has always loved antiques and old houses and was enchanted with this one. She had an easier trip to the Island than we did. She took the Skytrain to downtown and got on the bus to Victoria, which she had pre-booked. The bus went right on the ferry, then through to Victoria and one of the stops was about four blocks from the house where we were staying. The day we left we dropped her off at the bus stop and she got home the same way.

We did some extra sightseeing while she was there and did a favourite thing, we went to an Afternoon Tea at a Tea House, complete with tiny sandwiches, scones with cream and delicious desserts. It was a lovely visit that we all enjoyed.

Chapter 12

OUR LAST EXCHANGE, WITH A DIFFERENT TWIST

AFTER OUR VICTORIA EXCHANGE in 2011 we put our Homelink membership on hold because of medical issues. We planned to opt out for a year, then realized that I needed a second knee replacement, so we were actually out of the system for two years. We renewed our membership in 2015 but didn't specify any location. We thought we would just look at what was offered and look into anything that was really interesting.

That was the year that Homelink completely revamped their website and online listings. During this transition we got very few offers. The few we did get were not of interest to us.

That winter we went back to Hawaii for a month. While there, Doug commented on how nice it was to be in a warm place and how much he missed going to Australia, but he wasn't sure he could take the long 15-hour flight again. Another day, while on the same subject, he said that if he could get to Australia without flying, he'd love to go again.

Well… not long after we returned home, we saw advertised a cruise from Vancouver to Sydney. It was 28 days, leaving the last week in September, stopping at four ports in the Hawaiian Islands, three ports in Polynesia - Tahiti, Moorea and Bora Bora, and two ports in New Zealand before arriving in Australia. It was a cruise that appealed to us very much, so we agreed we'd do it, if we could find an exchange in Adelaide, one city we had only visited for short stops and hadn't spent much time in.

We sent out several inquiries to people in and around Adelaide and got a positive reply from a couple, Len and Judith, who said they lived just north of Adelaide on the oceanfront, and they had a boat we could also use. This interested us as Doug was in Sea Cadets as a young guy and learned to sail, but hadn't done much since. After a few e-mails we agreed to the exchange. Our ship would arrive in Sydney the last week in October, so we planned to stay in Sydney and visit with friends for a week and then go to Adelaide for three weeks. We told Len and Judith that they could come to our house for the month of October while we were on the ship, as well as the month we would be in Australia. They were pleased as their visit to BC would cover the nice fall weather with wine festivals, and far enough into November that they would most likely experience a snowfall. We then booked the cruise, booked a week at a boutique hotel in downtown Sydney and informed our Sydney friends of when we would be there.

We realized, of course, that we would have to fly back, but planned to break the long trip by stopping in Honolulu for a few days.

We corresponded with Len and Judith over the spring and summer and got to know them quite well. They planned to arrive two days before we left so we'd get to meet them.

About a month before the ship sailed things started to unravel.

First our Sydney friends e-mailed that they would not be in Sydney the week we were there. Their condo building was scheduled to have the elevator replaced and would be unavailable for use for about 10 days, spanning the time we were in Sydney. As he is in his 80s and she is almost there, and they live on the eighth floor, walking eight flights of stairs on a daily basis was not an option, so they decided to visit family in New Zealand during this time.

Although we were looking forward to seeing them and spending some time with them, it was not a big problem for us as Sydney is a city we know well. We decided we would buy the weekly transit pass we had before that enabled us to use the trains, busses, subways and harbor ferries.

The next problem was a medical one. I'd been experiencing some pain and difficulty walking over the summer and a visit to the doctor and an Xray, revealed that I had sciatica caused by a pinched nerve in my spine. Using a walker helped, but that posed a problem when travelling. On the ship wouldn't be a problem, but we had to fly to Adelaide, and we knew our exchange home was 20 miles outside the city and we would have to use trains and buses to get around. I realized I would probably be miserable most of the time, and it would put a burden on Doug as he would have to be responsible for carrying or dragging all our luggage. I knew it was more than I wanted to cope with right then.

So we made the decision not to go to Adelaide. Although we had planned to stay in Adelaide for three weeks, Len and Judith would only be in our house for two of those weeks as they planned to spend the third week in Vancouver. We decided we would stay in Sydney for one week, as planned, then fly to Honolulu and stay there for two weeks. Honolulu is also a city we know well and we booked a condo in the Ilikai hotel and condo complex, in an ocean front unit. We'd stayed there before and knew it was close to everything and easy to get wherever we wanted to go. I figured that if I didn't feel like doing anything I could always just sit on the balcony watching the beach and the boats, drinking Mai Tais and eating takeout.

We hadn't booked our flight yet, but we had planned to fly Hawaiian Air from Sydney to Honolulu. In the next few days, we informed Len and Judith of our decision, booked our flight to Honolulu and booked the condo in the Ilikai. This would be the second time that an exchange couple came to our house and we didn't go to theirs. As we had previously been to two exchanges that never came to ours, I guess it balanced out.

These changes would not be the only ones on this particular trip. We learned to take the good with the bad, change plans as we went and make the best of it.

One of the reasons I added this chapter is to let my readers know that things happen, plans change and it doesn't help to panic. Simply assess the problem, figure out what you can do to fix it and then do it. One of my mantras is: "If everything went right and according to plan and there were no problems, you'd have nothing to talk about later." As you can see, on some of our trips we had lots to talk about after.

Once we arrived at our ship, the Celebrity Solstice, and this part of the adventure began, we thoroughly enjoyed the experience. We did have a glitch in Sydney with the hotel we booked, but soon solved it, and even that turned out well.

One of the things we like to do on a cruise is play trivia, and as this cruise had a lot of sea days, we were looking forward to our trivia games. We always like to find partners from another country as they usually have different spheres of knowledge from us and this makes for a better team. This trip we partnered with two guys from Canberra, Australia, who were retired teachers. We made a good team and enjoyed their company.

Our first stop was Honolulu and then three other ports in Hawaii. We'd visited all the islands before, so in each port just got off the ship and walked around. In Honolulu we used our bus pass to get into town from the ship.

The Polynesia Islands were different. We had never been there before, so went on an island tour in all three ports. In Bora Bora we were fascinated to see the small thatched cottages on pilings in the water that are very expensive to rent. The transport here is called a Tuk Tuk and is an open bus with a roof but no sides. Not very comfortable, but great for taking photos.

We also stopped at two ports in New Zealand. The first port was a very rainy day, so we didn't get off the ship. The second port was Auckland, a city we'd been to before, so all we did here was go to a coffee shop that had wifi so we could pick up and answer e-mails.

Arriving in Sydney was spectacular. Sydney Harbour is one of the most beautiful in the world. We sailed into the harbour at dawn and watched the sun come up over the Opera House while eating breakfast. The ship docked very close to the famous Sydney Harbour Bridge and we could look up and see the cars carrying people into the city, and look down and see the harbour ferries packed with people also going to work.

We had booked a boutique hotel right in the downtown area near The Rocks, which is the official name of the waterfront area. The online description sounded just what we wanted: close to restaurants and stores, restaurant and pub on site, concierge service, large rooms with mini kitchens. We especially liked the kitchen as we prefer to do breakfasts and some lunches on our own.

The reality was anything but, plus a few surprises we hadn't planned on.

Unlike most hotels where the street and lobby are on the same level, this one had six steps leading to a landing with a door and then two more steps into the lobby. There was no one to help with luggage so we had to get our bags up these stairs and into the lobby by ourselves. The only way to do it was for one of us, me, to hold the door open while Doug carried all the luggage up the stairs. As it was only mid-morning, we knew we couldn't check in, but hoped we could store our luggage and go out. No such luck. There were already several people sitting around the lobby with piles of luggage looking unhappy. One of them told us that the storage room was already full from the people who had checked out earlier but had flights later in the day. Also, the restaurant wasn't open but the pub was. We got a coffee from the pub and sat down to wait. We got our room about 2 pm and didn't even look at it, just dropped our luggage, which we had to drag up there ourselves, and went out to find some lunch.

That was when we found out that we were in a business district full of tall office towers. Some of them had restaurants on the ground floor but they were packed with business lunch people. The couple of coffee shops had lines out the door. We finally found a restaurant two blocks away, ate lunch and then bought a couple of sandwiches and some fruit from their takeaway counter to have for dinner in our room.

Back in our room with a bag containing our dinner, we had another surprise. The advertised mini kitchen consisted of a tea set; china cups and saucers, cream and sugar containers (empty) 2 spoons and an electric kettle. No fridge, no microwave, no dishes, no supplies. With no refrigeration we opted to eat dinner in their restaurant. That's when we got the next surprise. The restaurant was closed and had been for quite some time. The pub offered to order takeout from a delivery service that we could eat there if we ordered drinks. We declined, went back to our room, ate the sandwiches we'd bought earlier and went to bed.

The next morning, I went to take a shower but couldn't open the glass door of the stall shower. Doug came in and yanked at it but he couldn't open it either. We did the best we could in the bathroom sink, which had no stopper in the outlet. On our way out to breakfast we told the person behind the front desk about the shower door and she promised to tell maintenance.

What we had planned to do today was buy our transit passes. On other trips we bought the overall pass that was good for everything, trains, buses, subway and harbour ferries. We tried to find out where the nearest ticket seller was located, but the desk clerk didn't know and the concierge desk was empty. We never did see anyone there. Someone on the street gave us directions to the bus depot, so we went there. There was a long lineup as it was the end of the month and people were buying their passes for the next month. When it was our turn, we got another surprise. They no longer sold passes for all modes of transport, but each one, busses, trains, ferries, etc, sold their own. That wouldn't work for us as we'd probably be better off paying individual fares as we went. By that time it had started to rain and we were quite wet from waiting in line. Also most of the restaurants had a queue outside for lunch. So we bought some more sandwiches form a takeaway counter and went back to our room.

Shortly after we got back the maintenance man came to look at the shower door. He couldn't get it open either and told us it was not repairable as the hinges were so corroded, they would need to be replaced and he didn't have any replacements. We called the desk to ask for another room and were told it was impossible as the hotel was full for the next few days with a conference group.

Here's where we sat down and had a serious talk. We were in a no-win situation and what could we do about it. We went on line with our laptop to see if we could find another hotel nearby and the first thing that popped up was the local forecast. The drizzle that had wet us in the bus ticket line had turned to a heavy downpour and the forecast said it would last for the next four or five days. So much for all the sightseeing we had planned.

Doug said, "I wish we were in Hawaii rather than here. This is the pits."

I said, "Then let's go. We have no reason to stay here. We can't go to the beach in the rain. We can't visit our friends. And if we don't have a shower for a week, they won't let us on the plane to go home."

So, we called Hawaiian Airlines and asked if we could move our flight booking to the next day. They said we could. Then we called the agency we'd booked the condo with in Honolulu and asked if we could have it five days earlier. They said we couldn't have the one we'd already booked but they had another in the same building, two floors higher and the same view that was available. We agreed that would be great. Lastly, we went to the front desk and told them we were leaving the next morning. They protested, saying we had booked for seven days and if we left, we still had to pay for the full week. We listed the shortcomings – the steps into the lobby with no help with luggage, the lack of a kitchen as promised, no concierge to help with planning, the closed restaurant, the non-working shower, and the last thing we mentioned was false advertising on the on-line booking sites. At that point they gave in and we only paid for two nights.

The next day we flew to Hawaii, checked into our oceanfront condo and had a great holiday in one of our favourite places.

About a week after we arrived back home, we received an e-mail from the hotel asking for a review. We couldn't believe they would actually ask, but we did it, outlining our experience. We subsequently received an e-mail from a man who said he was the new manager, that the hotel had changed hands, and he was appalled at what happened. He apologized and gave us reward points for the full seven days instead of the two we actually stayed. At least it gave us some insight into what had been going on.

At that point we felt that it was time to close the home exchanging phase of our lives. We had travelled far more than we ever thought we would, saw so many marvelous and different things, and enjoyed every minute of the adventure. Even the few problems we had; we didn't regret as they gave us something to talk about. And, as you just found out, also to write about.

There was no way we could have done what we did, see the things we saw, and met so many great people along the way if it hadn't been for home exchanging.

That cruise to Australia just might send us on a new path to adventure.

Printed in Canada